Noshe Djan
Afghan Food and Cookery

Picnicking in the Hindu Kush

Noshe Djan
Afghan Food and Cookery

by

Helen Saberi

with the help of
Najiba Zaka and Shaima Breshna

and drawings
by
Abdullah Breshna

PROSPECT BOOKS
1986

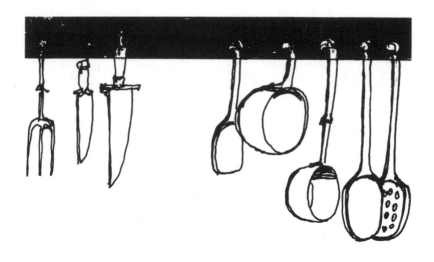

drawings © Abdullah Breshna, 1986

Published by Prospect Books, 45 Lamont Road, London SW10 OHU

Distributed in the U.S.A. by the University Press of Virginia,
Charlottesville, Virginia 22903

Design consultant Philip Wills

Set in 11 on 12 point Linotype Baskerville by Crypticks, Leeds

Printed and bound by Smith Settle, Otley, W. Yorks

At a time when thousands of Afghan freedom fighters are fearlessly fighting for their country and their beliefs, the author wishes to honour these brave people by quoting the following poem from Mr A. Baqi Qailzada, as a form of dedication.

As the translation shows, the poem has a double significance and a connection with food. Because of religious beliefs, only certain animals are acceptable to be slaughtered and eaten.

در صلح عشق جز نکو را نکشند
اگر مشتاقان زشت روز نکشند
که عاشق صادقی ز کشتن مگریز
مردار بود هر که آخر او را نکشند

It is only the beautiful and clean who are sacrificed at the altar of love; never the ugly and weak-natured.

If you are a true and devout lover, do not flinch from the sacrifice. It is only the unclean who are unworthy.

Map of Afghanistan

Contents

List of Illustrations

Acknowledgements

This book would not have been possible without the help and interest of many friends and relatives.

First of all I would like to thank my husband, Nasir, for all the help, advice, patience and especially encouragement he has given me in preparing this book. I must say he particularly enjoyed tasting all the recipes!

Special thanks are due to my sister-in-law, Najiba Zaka, and also my close friend, Shaima Breshna. Both sent me many recipes, but also advised and helped me with Afghan cooking techniques and traditions, and showed me how to make some of the more complicated dishes.

Special thanks too to Shaima's husband, Dip. Ing. Arch. Abdullah Breshna, for volunteering to provide all the lovely and unusual illustrations for the book.

Many other friends have given recipes, advice and encouragement. I should particularly like to thank Khalil and Sara Rashidzada, who invited us to their home to show me how to prepare the delicious speciality of the Uzbeks, *mantu*, and an Uzbek *pilau*. I am also grateful to Abdullah and Parwin Ali, Qassim and Valerie Hachimzai, Naheed and David Knight and Mr Abdul Ghaffour Redja.

I thank Anthony Hyman for his guidance and advice, particularly on the introduction; and Stephen Keynes for his help in getting the book published.

For so often looking after my children, especially baby Oliver, so that I could get on with the final testing of recipes and typing of the manuscript, I should like to express my gratitude to my mother, Hilda Canning, and my friends Carole Cooles and Louise Boyd. Young Alexander must also be thanked for his patience and understanding when I was too busy to help with homework or take him swimming.

Finally I would like to thank everyone at Prospect Books, especially Alan and Jane Davidson, not only for undertaking to publish this book and giving their expert advice, but also for their sympathy to the Afghan cause. I am particularly indebted to my copy-editor, Idonea Muggeridge, for her help and enthusiasm, all the more appreciated as I had never written a book before.

FURTHER READING

As the acknowledgments on the previous page show, I have learned from people rather than books, and I must say there are few books, in any language, which contain information about Afghan cookery. This short list includes some which I have consulted, and a couple which would be useful to anyone wishing to know more about Afghanistan.

AFGHANZADA, Abdullah: *Local Dishes of Afghanistan* (in Farsi): Kabul 1974.

DORJE, Rinjing: *Food in Tibetan Life:* Prospect Books, London, 1985.

DUPREE, Louis: *Afghanistan:* Princeton University Press, 1973. An encyclopaedic work.

HUSAIN, S. A.: *Muslim Cooking of Pakistan:* Sh. Muhammad Ashraf, Lahore, 1974.

JAFFREY, Madhur: *Indian Cookery:* BBC, London 1982.

MALOS, Tess: *Middle East Cookbook:* Summit Books, Sydney NSW, 1979 (has 20 pp on Afghanistan).

McKELLAR, Doris (compiled): *Afghan Cookery:* Afghan Book Publisher, Kabul, 1972.

MICHAUD, Roland and Sabrina: *Afghanistan:* Thames and Hudson, London, 1980. Many fine colour photographs.

RAMAZANI, Nesta: *Persian Cookery:* University Press of Virginia, 2nd printing, 1974.

REEJHSINGHANI, Aroona: *The Great Art of Mughlai Cooking:* Bell Books, New Delhi, 1979.

RODEN, Claudia: *A New Book of Middle Eastern Food:* Viking, London and New York, 1985.

WATT, George: *A Dictionary of the Economic Products of India*, vols 1-6: first published 1889, reprinted 1972 by Cosmo Publications, New Delhi.

WEIDENWEBER, Sigrid (compiled): *The Best of Afghan Cookery — an Afghan Recipe Book:* American Aid for Afghans, Portland, Oregon, 1980.

Author's Foreword

I became interested in Afghanistan at school after reading a book about the country and its culture and traditions. It sounded such a fascinating and interesting place that I became determined to visit it one day.

I had always been interested in foreign lands and had already travelled quite a bit. So after finishing school and secretarial college I applied for a job with the Foreign and Commonwealth Office. I worked first in London and then was posted to Warsaw. Soon after, I was posted from there to Kabul, Afghanistan. I was absolutely delighted and thrilled to be sent to one of the places where I had always wanted to go.

I arrived in Afghanistan in March 1971. I flew in a very small aeroplane from Peshawar to Kabul over the mountains and the famous Khyber Pass. It looked so barren, mountainous and dusty that I must admit I wondered if I had made a mistake in going there. However, after this somewhat daunting first impression I grew to love Afghanistan—its stark and stunning scenery, its barren and dusty deserts, the brilliant blue skies, snow clad mountains, lush green valleys, and the colourful and bustling bazaars; but most of all I loved it for the wonderful, hospitable people.

During my first year I travelled around the country as much as possible and met many Afghans including my future husband, and after a short engagement we were married in England in 1972. When we returned to live in Afghanistan, I was offered a locally-engaged post at the British Embassy. I had the best of both worlds—I kept my links with Britain, while at the same time I became an Afghan. I quickly learned the language of Dari, and during the next eight years travelled around most parts of the country. I became very interested in the culture and traditions of the people and in their food and customs.

We entertained a lot at home and even for our non-Afghan friends we nearly always cooked Afghan food. I have lots of happy and fond memories of hours spent in the kitchen with my maid, and also my friend, Gulbadan, and my mother-in-law,

11

preparing *ashak, boulanee, pilau,* and many other specialities and delicacies. I extended my knowledge of Afghan food and traditions in the best way possible, by being the guest of many families from different tribes and backgrounds and tasting all kinds of regional specialities on my travels.

I lived in Afghanistan until March 1980, when due to the Soviet invasion and occupation, the escalating fighting and civil disturbances, we decided reluctantly that it was time to leave. However, although we left most of our material belongings behind and some of our family and dear friends, I am fortunate still to have my memories, together with a tremendous love for Afghans and Afghanistan.

I often prepare Afghan food at home in London. My husband especially enjoys *ashak, pilau* dishes and kebabs. My nine year old son, Alexander, has a particular liking for *nan* and kebabs. When he smells *nan* baking, his eyes light up and he cannot wait for the bread to come out of the oven and to eat it while it is still warm and very fresh.

I decided to write this cookery book, not only because I think Afghan food will appeal to many people in the west, but, also because I felt that it would be a contribution, however small, to the Afghan cause. Afghanistan and the Afghans will not easily be forgotten. I also believe that it will be a valuable record of Afghan cookery and its rich, varied traditions which if the political situation does not change, may well be lost in a short time. The war is having terrible effects on the Afghan people, resulting in a massive exodus of refugees to countries all over the world and a consequent dispersal and destruction of their culture.

Many men, women and children are without food, medicines or shelter. An Afghan cookery book is perhaps especially poignant at the present time because there is a real threat of famine inside Afghanistan. Royalties from the sale of this book will go direct to charitable organisations working inside Afghanistan, to provide the food and medicines which are so desperately needed.

Helen Saberi
London, 1986

Introduction

Afghanistan is situated at the meeting place of four major cultural areas: the Middle East, Central Asia, the Indian subcontinent and the Far East. It is because of this geographical position that Afghanistan became the crossroads for many invading armies from different places each with their own culture. These marauding armies, often passing through Afghanistan, journeying further afield, realised the advantages of maintaining strongholds here and paused for a while.

In the fourth century BC, Alexander the Great conquered Afghanistan on his way to India; in the thirteenth and fourteenth centuries AD, Afghanistan was plundered by Genghis Khan and the Mongols en route to the Middle and Near East. Babur, founder of the Moghul Empire in India and a direct descendant of Genghis Khan, began his rise to power in Kabul and is buried in his favourite garden on a hill in Kabul, the Bagh-e-Babur Shah. The conqueror, Nader Shah Afshar invaded and conquered Afghanistan in the eighteenth century on his way to India recruiting Afghan fighters to serve with his troops. The British in India were twice invaders in the nineteenth century.

Afghan dynasties, in their turn, have flourished and at various times extended their influence to parts of Central Asia, India, Iran and even China. From the Kushans, to the Ghaznavid sultans, to the Durrani rulers such spheres of influence have contributed much to the rich patterns of civilisation.

Because of its special position in Central Asia, Afghanistan was also a crossroads on the ancient Silk Routes connecting Europe with the Far East. Traders and merchants from many

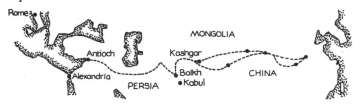

countries travelled there, including the famous Venetian traveller Marco Polo. This traffic brought many imported items such as Chinese tea and Indian spices, all of which have had a big effect on Afghan cuisine.

The numerous different ethnic groups living in Afghanistan —the Tajiks, Turkomans, Uzbeks, Baluchis, Pashtuns and Hazaras are just some of them—have also left their mark on Afghan traditions and food.

In short, Afghanistan has been a melting pot for a large number of cultures and traditions over the centuries, and these different influences can be detected in the variety of Afghan food and the regional specialities. Readers of this book will find many similarities with Greek, Turkish, Middle Eastern, Persian, Central Asian, Indian and even Far Eastern foods and dishes.

CLIMATE

Afghanistan is a land of contrasts—vast areas of scorching parched deserts, large areas of high, cold and inaccessible mountains and extensive green plains and valleys, some of which are sub-tropical. Generally the summers are dry and very hot and the winters very cold with heavy snowfalls especially in the mountains. It is this snow which provides the much needed water for irrigation in the late spring and summer. The plains and valleys are very fertile so long as there is water, and a wide variety of crops can be cultivated; it is these crops which determine the everyday diet of Afghans.

Cereals such as wheat, corn, barley and even rice are the chief crops. Rice is grown on the terraces of the Hindu Kush in the north and in the Jalalabad area. Cotton is grown in the north and south west of the country, and cotton factories in Kunduz and Lashkargah produce edible cottonseed oil. Sugar beet is grown mainly in the Pule Khumri/Kunduz area and is processed in the factory at Pule Khumri. Sugar cane is cultivated in the Jalalabad/Nangarhar area.

Because the range of climatic conditions in Afghanistan is so wide, a great variety of vegetables and fruits grow in abundance. Afghanistan is particularly famous for its grapes, from which green and red raisins are produced, and for its melons.

SOCIAL CUSTOMS AND TRADITIONS

Afghanistan is a poor country but it is rich in traditions and social customs. Unfortunately it is not possible to describe the Afghan way of life in great detail in this book, but I have endeavoured to pick out the most interesting and important aspects relating to food and cookery.

Hospitality is very important in the Afghan code of honour. The best possible food is prepared for guests even if other members of the family have to go without. A guest is always given a seat or the place of honour at the head of the room. Tea is served first to the guest to quench his thirst. While he is drinking and chatting with his host, all the women and girls of the household are involved in the preparation of food.

The traditional mode of eating in Afghanistan is on the floor. Everyone sits around on large colourful cushions, called *toshak*. These cushions are normally placed on the beautiful carpets, for which Afghanistan is famous. A large cloth or thin mat called a *disterkhan* is spread over the floor or carpet before the dishes of food are brought. In summer, food is often served outside in the cooler night air, or under a shady tree during the day. In the depth of winter food is eaten around the *sandali*, the traditional form of Afghan heating. A *sandali* consists of a low table covered with a large duvet called a *liaf* which is also big enough to cover the legs of the occupants, sitting on their cushions or mattresses and supported by large pillows called *balesht* or *poshty*. Under the table is a charcoal brazier called a *mankal*. The charcoal has to be thoroughly burned previously and covered with ashes.

Food is usually shared communally; three or four people will share one large platter of rice and individual side dishes of stew *qorma*, or vegetables. Home made chutneys, pickles, as well as fresh *nan* usually accompany the food.

The traditional way of eating is with the right hand, and with no cutlery. Spoons may be used for puddings and teaspoons for tea. Because hands are used in eating there is a handwashing ceremony before meals and for this a special bowl and jug called a *hoftawa-wa-lagan* is used. A young boy or girl member of the family brings this to the guest, and pours the water over his hands for him, the bowl being used to catch the water.

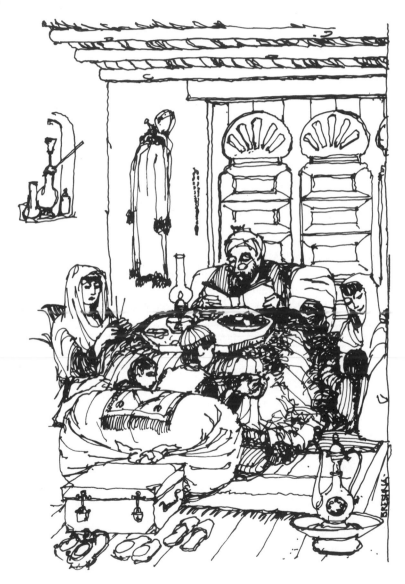

SANDALI

THE MOST ECONOMICAL AFGHAN SYSTEM OF HEATING

MANKAL = CHARCOAL CONTAINER

SANDALI = TABLE

LIAF = SQUARE BLANKET

TAKHTA = STONE OR WOOD PLATE

TOSHAK = COTTON MATTRESS

BALESHT OR POSHTY = CUSHION

AFTABA - LAGAN

*The handwashing
ceremony and the*
haftawa-wa-lagan

SPECIAL OCCASIONS AND RELIGIOUS FESTIVALS

Afghanistan is a Muslim country and religion plays a very important part in the way of life. Afghans observe all religious days and festivals, which are based on the lunar calendar.

The two most important festivals are *Eid-ul-Fitr* (also called *Eid-e-Ramazan*) and *Eid-e-Qorban* (sometimes called *Eid-ul-Adha*).

Eid-ul-Fitr, which goes on for three days, marks the end of *Ramazan*, the month of fasting, and is celebrated rather like our Christmas. Children receive new clothing and families visit relatives and friends. Presents are not exchanged but in recent years the practice of sending Eid cards has increased considerably.

Eid-e-Qorban is the major festival marking the end of the *Haj*, the pilgrimage to Mecca, and lasts for four days. Again, children receive new clothing and friends and relatives are visited.

At each *Eid*, tea, nuts, sweets and sugared almonds called *noqle* are served to visitors and guests. Often special sweets and pastries are also prepared; *halwa-e-swanak*, *sheer payra*, *goash-e-feel* and others. Many Afghans sacrifice a lamb or calf at *Eid-e-Qorban*, which takes its name from the word *qorban*, meaning sacrifice. The meat is distributed among the poor, relatives and neighbours.

Another important day of celebration is New Year, called *Nauroz*. The Afghan New Year falls on 21 March, the spring equinox, our first day of spring. This special day, which celebrates new life, has its origins long before Islam, in the time of Zoroaster and the Zoroastrians, who worshipped fire. Special dishes and foods are made for the New Year: *kulcha Naurozee*, a biscuit made with rice flour and sometimes called *kulcha birinji*; and *miwa Naurozee*, a fruit and nut compote, also called *haft miwa* or *haft seen* by some because it contains seven (*haft*) fruits and the name of each fruit includes the Persian letter *seen*. *Shola-e-shireen*, a sweet rice dish, is also made on this day for *Nazer*, a kind of thanksgiving (see p 22). Another traditional food at this time is *sabzi chalau* with chicken. The recipes for these dishes can be found in the relevant chapters.

Samanak is another ancient dish prepared especially for New Year. About fifteen to twenty days before the New Year, wheat is planted in flower pots and from this wheat a sweet pudding is made. The preparation for this dish is elaborate.

At New Year when everything is new and fresh and the bitter winter is finally over, Afghans like to go on picnics and many people visit holy shrines, *ziarat*.

Buzkashi is also played at New Year. It is the country's

national sport and it resembles polo. *Buzkashi* literally means 'goat-grabbing'. The headless body of a goat, or sometimes a calf, is used in place of a ball. The game originated on the plains of Kunduz and Mazar-i-Sharif during the time of the Mongol invasions of Afghanistan, when it is said that the Mongol horsemen used (decapitated) prisoners of war instead of goats.

Children go out to fly their kites. These are made with colourful tissue paper on a light wooden frame, and the thread, specially made with ground glass, is extremely sharp. The kites fight each other in the air, trying to cut the thread of other kites.

Afghans love an excuse for a party. Births, circumcisions, engagements and weddings are celebrated in grand style, although many of the associated customs are dying out.

The birth of a child, especially the first male child is a big occasion, when many guests will be expected. Numerous dishes and specialities are prepared; *aush, ashak, boulanee,* kebabs, *pilau* and many desserts. Celebrations continue for ten days. On the third day or sometimes the sixth day, called *Shab-e-shash,* the local priest, *mullah,* comes to bless the child and the naming ceremony takes place. Relatives sit round a room and choose a name which is then called into the baby's ear. On the tenth day (*dah*) after the birth, the mother gets up for the first time (until this time her women relatives have been looking after her and the baby) and goes to the public baths (*hamam*). This day is therefore called *Hamam-e-dah. Humarch,* a flour-based soup, or *aush* and *shola-e-olba,* the sweet rice dish with fenugreek, are made especially on this day. On the 40th day after the birth, the sweet bread called *roht* is baked for close family relatives. *Roht* is also baked and rolled on the day the child walks for the first time.

Circumcision is another occasion which is still celebrated. Relatives and friends gather together when the male child is circumcised. Traditionally, the local barber is responsible for performing this task. On such a day kebabs are made from the fresh meat of a lamb specially sacrificed for the occasion and are served with a variety of foods.

Engagements and weddings are elaborate and many of the celebrations vary between the different ethnic groups. They also vary from city to village. Any engagement or wedding is an occasion for a large party.

Engagements are called *shirnee khoree*, which literally means sweet eating. Traditionally the family of the groom bring sweets, *goash-e-feel*, presents, clothes, jewellery and other gifts for the bride's family. The bride's family in return prepares and organises the food and the party to celebrate the occasion. Large numbers of guests, depending on the social standing and financial circumstances of the bride's family are invited. Special kitchens are often set up in order to cope with the preparation of vast amounts of food; *pilau, qorma, ashak, boulanee* and many varieties of desserts; *firni, shola,* jellies, pastries and of course lots of fruit. The tea *qymaq chai* is usually served.

Weddings take place in two stages: *nikah,* the religious cere-mony when the marriage contract is actually signed, takes place first and is followed by *arusi,* which is a combination of wedding party and further ceremony.

At the second stage of the wedding the guests are first served with food while the bride is preparing herself in a separate room. A wide assortment of rich dishes similar to those at an engagement are served. The *arusi* ceremony usually takes place quite late in the evening and after the inevitable tea.

The bride and bridegroom are then brought together for the first time (the bride was not present at the religious ceremony—her signing of the contract was done by proxy). The groom sits on a raised platform called *takht* (throne) and the bride approaches, heavily veiled with female relatives holding the *Qor'an* (Koran) over her head. The bride joins the groom and a mirror is placed before them. Several ceremonies then take place involving the tasting of *sharbat* (sherbert) and *malida,* a flour-based, powdery sweet. Henna is painted on the couple's hands or fingers. Sugared almonds (*noqle*) and other sweets are then showered over the newly-weds, rather like the western tradition of throwing confetti.

Another less happy occasion when many friends and relatives get together is for a death. Food is prepared for the mourning family and guests, many of whom will stay for a number of days with the bereaved family. On the first Friday after a death, and on the 40th day, relatives and friends gather together to hear the *Qor'an* being read, usually by the local priest (*mullah*), after which food is served.

Another custom which perhaps should be mentioned here is the *Shab-e-mourdaha*, which literally means night of the dead. These special nights are held on the eve of an *Eid* and New Year. The dead of the family are remembered and *halwa* is made and distributed to the poor.

Nazer is another important religious custom. It is practised by all, whether rich or poor, and is similar to a thanksgiving, but can take place on any day. *Nazer* is offered for a number of reasons like the safe return of a relative after a journey or recovery from a serious illness. Another important reason for *nazer* is to mark a visit to a holy shrine and the fulfilment of a prayer made on this pilgrimage. For these occasions special dishes such as *halwa* or *shola* are cooked and distributed to the poor. The most simple offering for *nazer* is to buy a dozen fresh *nan* and hand pieces out to passers-by in the street. The more affluent sacrifice a lamb or calf. *Nazer* is always accepted graciously as it has such religious significance.

My mother-in-law used to make a large pot of *halwa*. Portions of this were placed on a large piece of fresh *nan*. A large tray was set up and a servant or member of the family went out on to the street and offered it to anyone passing by. We also sent it to our neighbours.

Nazer is also held on other important religious days such as the birthday of Prophet Mohammad or on the tenth day of *Muharram* (the lunar month of mourning) which is the anniversary of the massacre of Hazrat-e-Hussein, grandson of Mohammad and seventy two members of his family. There is also *Nazer Bibi*, Bibi being Fatima El-Zahiza, the daughter of Prophet Mohammad. On this occasion, rice or wheat *halwa* is served on round thin bread cooked in oil.

Of course, some traditions and customs have disappeared, especially in the cities. The towns and cities have become increasingly westernised, particularly the capital, Kabul. Tables and chairs are now in common use, as is cutlery, although knives are still not used much. Buffet meals are often prepared for large parties.

There is no special order for serving Afghan food and usually at a large party the table is set with all the main dishes; *pilau*, *qorma*, vegetables and salads are placed together with the desserts and fruits. It is up to the individual to choose whether to eat each dish separately or to eat all the dishes on one plate. However, the desserts are eaten last and followed by fruit. After every meal tea is served. Enormous amounts of food are prepared on special occasions. Second helpings are a must if you are not to offend your host. Often the host or hostess will come round and serve you with a large extra helping, insisting that you eat more of this or that delicacy.

Left-overs from these feasts are never wasted. There are always willing eaters in the kitchen who have been involved in the preparation of the food and who wait until the guests have finished. What they cannot manage can always be eaten the next day.

Afghans rarely eat in restaurants. There were a few restaurants in Kabul and in other large towns but these mostly catered for foreigners and travellers. *Chaikhana*, teahouses, on the other hand, are very popular and Afghans go there to meet their friends, exchange gossip and sit and drink tea. Food can be bought but it is mainly for travellers. Afghans do like to eat kebabs which are prepared at kebab stalls and they also buy snacks from street vendors known as *tawaf* or *tabang wala*. A *tabang wala* carries his food and utensils balanced on his head on a large, flat, round wooden tray called a *tabang*. He sets up a stall wherever or whenever appropriate, sometimes staking a claim to a particular street corner. He provides an assortment of food such as *jelabi*, *pakaura*, sliced boiled potatoes with vinegar, boiled chick peas or kidney beans served with vinegar and boiled eggs.

A popular game played by children at *Eid* or *Nauroz* resembles our Easter custom of coloured eggs. The eggs are brightly decorated in different colours and the game consists in knocking together two boiled eggs with a friend. The owner of the egg whose shell cracks first is the loser. Sometimes a *tabang wala* sells dried fruits and nuts, fruit and nut compotes such as *kishmish ab* (raisins in water), and sweets.

Another game which both adults and children play involves the pulling and breaking of a chicken wishbone. Very often at a party a *pilau* with chicken will be specially cooked as an excuse to play this game. Unlike the game played with a wishbone in the west, it does not matter who receives the larger piece; the pulling of the wishbone simply marks the start of a game between two players, on which bets, usually for another party or money or clothing, will be placed. At any time after the wishbone has been pulled one of the players may try to win by handing an object, of any nature, to the other. The one who receives the object must remember that the game has been set in motion and must say *Mara yod ast* (I remember). The game goes on until one player forgets and becomes the loser. The winner marks his victory by saying *Mara yod ast, tura feramush* (I remember, you forget).

With the arrival of snow, the adults play a game called *barfi*, which also involves the giving of a party. A friend or relative sends a note in an envelope containing some of the first snow. It is usually delivered by a servant or a child. If you unsuspectingly accept the envelope you must pay the forfeit by giving a party for the sender and his family. Some Afghans take care to avoid answering the door during the first snowfall, but many will await the deliverer, for, if you can catch the person delivering the note, the tables are turned and it is the sender who must give the party. When this happens the deliverer has a black mark made with charcoal on his forehead or his hands are tied behind his back and then he is returned in disgrace to the sender's house. I was once caught out by one of my husband's young cousins. I think his family took unfair advantage of a foreigner who was not well versed in Afghan traditions!

A favourite pastime is a picnic called *maila*, especially in spring and summer, although in peacetime the people of Kabul went for picnics even in winter, sometimes an extended one lasting the whole weekend, down in the warmer climes of Jalalabad. In summer, picnickers would go to the cooler mountain regions of Paghman or the Salang in the Hindu Kush. In spring the picturesque village of Istalif and the lake at Sarobi were favourite haunts.

In true Afghan style, mountains of food were taken and

prepared on the spot for these picnics. A fire would be lit and kebabs or fish grilled over charcoal and served with salads and hot fresh *nan*, bread. Sometimes the more adventurous would cook *pilau*. Afterwards tea was brewed and everyone would relax and enjoy the fresh air. Some Afghan picnics are quite lively affairs, and there is music and dancing for the more energetic. People bring their own musical instruments, or popular Indian dance music on tape.

Some foods and desserts are prepared only at certain seasons. In spring or early summer, *faluda* is made. This is a milk custard mixed with snow brought down from the mountains in large blocks, sugar, pistachios and rose-water. Locally made ice cream *sheer yakh* belongs to the same season. *Kishmish panair* is another traditional food found only in the spring: a white uncured cheese served with red raisins. Winter is the season for the speciality called *haleem*, a dish of wheat mixed with ground meat and served with oil and sugar, usually bought from the bazaar. Winter is also the time for fish and *jelabi*.

In the fish bazaar

25

An Afghan kitchen

The Afghan Kitchen

The traditional Afghan kitchen is very basic. Few people have ovens, even in the cities. Most of the cooking is done over wood or charcoal fires, and many would say that Afghan food tastes much better if cooked thus. Some Afghans do, however, have a clay oven (*tandoor*), used for baking their own bread.

Refrigerators are rare. To keep food cool and fresh in the hot summers, Afghans use a range of clay pots and containers shown in the drawings on page 28.

There is usually no running water. All washing up is done outside, using a well.

WEIGHTS AND MEASURING

Afghans rarely measure out their ingredients like people in western countries. Recipes tend to be passed down from mother to daughter and learned through practice and experience. Most kitchens do, however, have a range of pots with handles called *malaqa*, which are used as measuring aids, and ordinary cups and glasses are also used for measuring.

Weights are of course used in buying food. Those used are the *seer, charak, pow, khord* and *misqal*. The last is the smallest and is used for weighing gold and spices. The equivalences in the metric system are as follows:

1 *seer* = 7 kg
1 *charak* = 1/4 *charak* = 1.75 kg
1 *pow* = 1/4 *charak* = 438g
1 *khord* = 1/4 *pow* = 109 g
1 *misqal* = 1/24 *khord* = 4.5 g

I remember being amazed the first time I bought some fruit from a 'donkey seller' (trader with a donkey, not selling donkeys) in the fruit bazaar. He took his hand scales and put the fruit on one end and a stone on the other! This stone represented 1 *pow*. Some foreigners who could not believe that they were being given the correct weight would rush to the nearest shop and ask them to weigh the goods with 'proper' scales and weights. In fact, the hand scales were always accurate, but I never saw any of these poor donkey sellers getting annoyed or upset by this insult to their honesty. They just used to smile and shrug their shoulders.

COOKS AND EQUIPMENT

Cooking is normally done by the female members of the family although for big occasions and parties professional male cooks are hired. The men of the family are usually responsible for the shopping. Family is a much broader concept in the East. It does not refer only to immediate relatives. The size of the Asian 'extended family' means that a large amount of food must be prepared each day and this takes up a considerable time.

Food tends to be cooked slowly and for a longer time so that the full flavours of the ingredients are brought out. Often a *pilau* will taste better warmed up the next day.

The methods of preparation are extensive and laborious, and sophisticated kitchen equipment such as electric food processors or grinders are practically non-existent. However, most families do have a range of simple kitchen utensils and equipment. In the list which follows I indicate where more modern devices can be substituted.

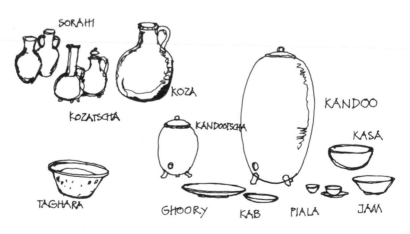

DAYG: pans
Afghan cooks use a collection of various copper pans, lined with an alloy which I believe contains zinc. Pans are named after the weight of rice which can be cooked in them. For example, *dayg-e-yak seera* is a pan used for cooking 1 *seer* (7 kg) of rice. Pans range in size from just under 1 lb, *dayg-e-yak pow*, up to 10 *seer* (70 kg), *dayg-e-dah seera*. Cast iron pans are also used and recently aluminium pans have been introduced, but copper pans remain the most popular.

For cooking Afghan dishes, especially a *pilau*, I would recommend using heavy, thick-bottomed cast iron pans, which prevent sticking and burning. It is also a good idea to have a heavy bottomed pan without a handle which can double up as a casserole for cooking in the oven. Pans in Afghanistan do not have handles and so can be used both on top of the stove and in the oven.

AWANG: pestle and mortar
All Afghan homes have a pestle and mortar, usually a brass one. They are essential for crushing garlic and onions and grinding herbs and spices. However, an electric grinder is a much quicker way of grinding spices, but take care to clean it after use. I sometimes use a garlic press for crushing garlic.

AWANG

MACHINE-E-GOSHT: mincer
Most Afghans possess their own mincer, as they mince their own meat for the preparation of *qima*, minced meat, *kofta*, meatballs and some kebabs. They also use a mincer for shredding onions. To save time, a food processor can be used. In the old days in Afghanistan, before the modern mincer, meat was chopped up finely in the bazaar by the butcher, using a large chopper on a large wooden log.

KAFGEER: large slotted spoon
A long handled utensil used for stirring dishes and for serving rice. The head of a *kafgeer* is round, flat and slotted. An ordinary large slotted spoon makes a good substitute.

MALAQA: measuring pot
A range of pots with handles called *malaqa* are used for measuring out such things as flour and rice. Ordinary scales in metric or imperial weights can be used for the recipes in this book, along with a measuring jug for liquid measurements.

AUSH GAZ: rolling pin
To roll out dough for pasta dishes and some of their sweet pastries, Afghans use an *aush gaz*. This is a long, thin wooden stick, similar to a rolling pin.

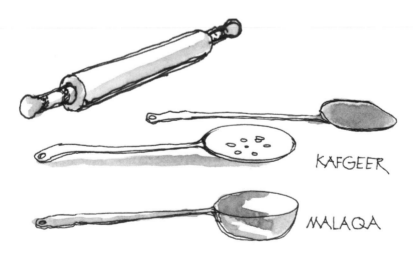

KAFGEER

MALAQA

CHALAU SOF: colander
A colander is used not only for washing and draining vegetables but for draining rice. *Chalau sof* literally means drained white rice.

DAYG-E-BOKHAR: steamer
This is the name for the steamer used for making the Uzbek dish of *mantu*. However, nowadays many Afghans possess pressure cookers and these are also called *dayg-e-bokhar*. *Bokhar* means steam in Dari.

MANKAL: barbecue (charcoal brazier)
For cooking small amounts of soup or frying eggs or just boiling water many Afghans use a *mankal*. This is a small round iron device for cooking over charcoal, rather like a barbecue.

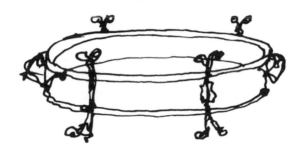

SIKH: skewers
Skewers are necessary for cooking some of the kebabs in this book. If you have a charcoal barbecue so much the better.

TAGHORA-E-KHAMIRI: mixing bowl
A large clay bowl used for kneading dough. An ordinary mixing bowl is perfectly adequate. Most Afghan kitchens also have a *taghora-e-qurooti*, the special bowl used for reconstituting *quroot*, dried, drained yoghurt (p 38).

INGREDIENTS AND TECHNIQUES

All the ingredients used in this book can be bought either in supermarkets, delicatessens or in Asian grocery shops.

Afghan food uses a wide variety of herbs and spices, with results which are neither too hot and spicy nor too bland. Spices and herbs, apart from flavouring the food, have medicinal properties and therefore many of them are used to aid the digestion or for other medicinal purposes.

SPICES

Ideally spices should be bought whole and they will stay fresh for long periods if stored in cool, dry, dark places in tightly lidded jars. Spices can be ground with a pestle and mortar or in an electric coffee grinder. Care must be taken that the grinder is thoroughly cleaned beforehand and afterwards so that no cross-flavouring occurs. One way to do this is to wipe the grinder out with kitchen paper and then grind one or two slices of stale bread. It is also a good idea, if you use certain spices frequently, to use pepper mills for grinding them, one mill for each specific spice. Most Afghans have a special mill for grinding cardamom, which they use frequently in cooking and also add to their tea.

Below I have listed alphabetically the spices most commonly used and which appear in the recipes in this book. The Afghan name is shown after the English one.

ANISEED: *bodiyan*
It is used for flavouring savoury biscuits and the bread called *roht*, and also medicinally as an aid to digestion and to ease flatulence, and for babies to relieve wind. Dill seed can be substituted.

BLACK CUMIN SEED, see under KALONJI

CARDAMOM: *ail*
It is the seeds which form the spice. There are three types of cardamom: green, white, and black, according to the colour of the pods containing the seeds. The green and white cardamom are used in Afghan cooking for *pilau*, desserts and in black or green tea. The flavour is strong and spicy. The green and white pods are sometimes chewed whole to relieve indigestion and to sweeten the breath. The black pods are even stronger.

Grinding spices

CHILLIES: *murch-e-sabz, murch-e-surkh*

Chillies, from the capsicum family, are 'hot' and must be handled carefully—they contain an irritant which can burn your skin, so always wash your hands after using them. In the Afghan kitchen they appear in two forms.

Murch-e-sabz are the long, fresh, green chillies, rich in vitamins A and C. Afghans like to nibble these with their food, but they are also added whole to give flavour to soups and stews, or chopped and put in kebabs, salads, chutneys and pickles.

Murch-e-surkh are dried red chillies, to be used sparingly. They are sometimes added to soups and stews. Ground, they become hot red pepper.

CINNAMON: *dal chini*

Cinnamon is the inner bark of the tree *Cinnamomum zehlanicum*, a member of the large laurel family. It can be bought in 'stick' (a thin roll, better called a 'quill') or ground form. Sometimes the sticks are used whole in stews, but ground cinnamon is more common and goes into the mixture called 'four spices'.

CLOVES: *mikhak*
These are the dried flower buds of the shrub *Syzygium aromaticum*. The name comes from the Latin *clovus*, meaning nail, and in fact *mikhak* also means little nail in Dari. Ground cloves are usually one of the spices in *char marsala* (see 'four spices').

CORIANDER SEEDS: *tokhum-e-gashneetch*
The seeds of the coriander plant form a spice, while its leaves are a herb (see p 36). The seeds can be bought whole or ground and are used mainly for flavouring meatballs and stews. Their flavour is spicy and sweet, but mild.

CUMIN: *zeera*
A strong, slightly bitter spice which is used with long grain rice. It is also used as an aid to digestion, and is one of the 'four spices' described further on.

DILL SEED: *tokhum-e-shabit*
The seeds from the feathery herb, dill, are sometimes used as a substitute for aniseed (*bodiyan*).

FENUGREEK: *olba*
This is used for flavouring spinach and the sweet rice dish *shola-e-olba* (p 132). The seeds, which are rich in vitamins and sugar, are also used for some pickles such as *turshi limo* (lemon pickle).

FOUR SPICES: *char marsala*
A combination of four spices which are ground together in equal parts and used to flavour *pilau*. Although the choice varies from family to family, the four are usually cinnamon, cloves, cumin and black cardamom seeds. This combination of spices derives from the *garam masala* of India.

GINGER: *zanja feel* (meaning yellow elephant)
In Afghanistan it is used for flavouring turnip and cauliflower, but its main use is medicinal, as an aid to digestion.

KALONJI: *sia dona*
The small black seeds which can be bought from Asian groceries under this name are needed in many recipes. They come from the plant *Nigella sativa*, and are sometimes called nigella seeds, but not in the shops. They are a confusing item because some people call them 'black onion seeds', although they have nothing to do with onions. It is also wrong to call them 'black cumin seeds', as true cumin seeds come from a different plant. However, I have used this name in the recipes, as it seems to be the most common English one. The seeds have an earthy aroma and are often sprinkled on *nan* and savoury biscuits before these are baked. They are also used in pickling.

PEPPER, BLACK: *murch-e-sia*
This is used liberally in Afghan dishes.

PEPPER, RED: *murch-e-surkh*
Made from dried red chillies, this is called 'red chilli powder' by Asian grocers. It is like cayenne pepper. On the whole Afghan food is not very hot, but some dishes do require a small amount of this. It has digestive properties and is rich in vitamin C.

POPPY SEED: *khosh khosh*
Poppies grow abundantly in Afghanistan and their seeds, whether white or black, are free of opium (as are the seeds of all poppies). The seeds have a nutty flavour and are sometimes sprinkled on bread or savoury biscuits.

SAFFRON: *zaffaron*
Saffron is a very expensive spice which gives a strong flavour, scent and colour to dishes. It is often used to colour *pilau* and in desserts but, because it costs so much, Afghans often substitute turmeric or yellow food colouring which they call *rang-e-shireen*, literally meaning 'sweet colour'. For rice desserts they use this substitute. Other ways of colouring *pilau* are to add ground, browned onions or caramelised sugar.

SESAME SEEDS: *done kunjid*
These have a lovely nutty flavour and are often sprinkled on breads before baking, or ground to make sesame seed oil.

TURMERIC: *zar choba*
Turmeric, which is closely related to ginger, has a mild earthy flavour and is used for flavouring and giving a yellow colour to *pilau*, soups and stews. It is also an aid to digestion.

HERBS

CORIANDER: *gashneetch*
This is my favourite herb and is also very popular in Afghanistan. It is sometimes called Afghan parsley because it is used just like parsley, for garnishing as well as for flavour. It is added to soups, meatballs and salads. The taste of fresh coriander is delightful and gives a lovely flavour to food. It can be stored successfully in the refrigerator if put in an airtight container in its unwashed state. The seeds are a spice.

DILL: *shabit*
This feathery herb, with a piquant flavour, is a member of the same family as parsley. It is mainly used to flavour soups, some rice dishes and spinach. The seeds are a spice.

GARLIC: *seer*
Garlic is very popular, both as a flavouring and for medicinal purposes. It is said to tone up the digestive system.

MINT: *nana, pudina*
A popular herb. *Nana* is the common or garden mint, but the kind called *pudina* is specially liked. I am told it is *Mentha pulegium*, also known as pennyroyal.

PULSES

Many different kinds of pulses are used; they help to provide protein and vitamin B when meat is not readily available. Apart from their food value, pulses are versatile and are used in many soups, rice and meat dishes.

All pulses should be picked over and washed. Whole beans should be soaked overnight in water before cooking. Cooking time depends on the freshness of the pulses; fresh pulses cook more quickly. The best time to add salt is halfway through the cooking time as salt tends to slow down the softening.

Below I have listed those pulses which are regularly used and can be obtained easily.

CHICKPEAS: *nakhud*
These are mainly added to soups, such as *aush*.

MUNG BEANS: *maush*
Mung beans are small, green, oval shaped beans used to make bean sprouts in Oriental cooking. In Afghanistan they are used in short grain rice dishes such as *shola goshti* and in the soup, *maushawa*. If you cannot find them, substitute green lentils.

RED KIDNEY BEANS: *lobiya*
These are large, dark red kidney-shaped beans. They are used in soups and meat dishes.

SPLIT PEAS: *dal nakhud*
Yellow split peas are also popular. They are used in stews, *qorma*. When cooking these peas, leave the lid slightly ajar as a thick froth forms during cooking and can boil over. The froth should be skimmed off.

MOONG DAL: *dal*
This *dal* is the skinned and split version of the green mung beans used in dishes such as *maushawa* and *shola*. The grains are pale yellow and slightly elongated. The word *dal* applies both to the split beans and to the dish made with them, which originated in India (where there are countless kinds of dal).

OTHER INGREDIENTS

Below I give details of other ingredients, and the techniques associated with them, which are important in the Afghan kitchen.

VEGETABLE OIL: *roghan-e-naboti*
Traditionally Afghans cooked with what is called *roghan-e-dumbah*, a lard rendered from the tail of the fat-tailed sheep. However, the more wealthy used *roghan-e-zard*, a clarified butter, often called *ghee* (as in India). The use of vegetable shortening and vegetable oil has increased in recent years with imports from Pakistan, India, Iran and Western Europe. Also, two local factories at Lashkargah and Kunduz produce vegetable oil.

I have used vegetable oil for the recipes in this book. Ground-nut oil, corn oil and sunflower oil are all suitable.

Afghan tastes favour a large amount of fat or oil and in fact this is also a sort of status symbol. If you are wealthy you can afford more cooking oil. I have taken western tastes into account while preparing the recipes, but the amount of oil or fat used can be further adjusted; and any unwanted oil can always be spooned off just before serving.

YOGHURT: *mast*

A lot of live, natural yoghurt (i.e. containing cultures) is eaten and used in Afghan cooking. This sort should be used in the recipes.

Many recipes call for *chaka*, a thick, creamy substance made by draining yoghurt in a cheesecloth or muslin bag for about an hour. If you neglect to drain the yoghurt, the whey left in it may give your dishes a slightly bitter taste. But you can buy yoghurt already strained, like the Greek strained yoghurt which I use.

Chaka is often salted and dried and formed into round balls, called *quroot*. They look rather like white pebbles and are quite hard. For use in cooking they are reconstituted in water in a special bowl called a *taghora qurooti*. Afghans sometimes add to this garlic, salt and pepper, then boil it and eat it with *nan*. For added flavour they sprinkle dried mint on top.

AFGHAN 'CLOTTED CREAM': *qymak*

Qymak is a milk product which has some resemblance to clotted cream and is clearly a close relation of the *kaymak* of the Middle East. It can be bought from dairy shops in Afghanistan or prepared at home. The way of making it is to take cow's or goat's milk, boil it to reduce it, and then leave it for some hours so that the thick layer forms on top. A very little cornflour is sprinkled on top of the hot milk when the boiling is completed, and this assists the formation of the layer, which is so thick as to be almost solid. A bowl of *qymak* with *nan* is often enjoyed for breakfast, but it is better known in *qymak chai* (p 152), a green tea prepared in a special way with *qymak* floating on top.

ONIONS: *piaz*

Onions are essential in the Afghan kitchen, and two types are used, red and white. The red onions are used for cooking as they

Draining yoghurt to make chaka

give a thicker sauce and a richer flavour. The white onions are more commonly used in salads.

It is important that onions are fried properly. Use plenty of oil and start the frying on a medium to high heat, turning it down a little as the onions begin to brown, lose water and become soft. If the onions are fried too hard they will not dissolve and the sauce will be watery and weak in colour. Afghans use plenty of onions to make their sauces, as the more onions, the thicker and richer the sauce.

CHINESE CHIVES: *gandana*
A green from the leek family which looks rather like long grass and is usually called 'Chinese chives' in western countries. It is used in many dishes such as *ashak* and *boulanee* and with spinach. Unless you grow your own, *gandana* may be difficult to obtain, so leeks (which have a similar taste) may be used.

TOMATOES: *bonjon-e-rhumi*
Tomatoes are used to flavour and colour meat dishes and soups and of course they are eaten raw on their own and in salads. In the summer months, when tomatoes are cheap and plentiful, tomato paste and chutneys are made at home for use during the winter months. Where the recipes in this book use tomatoes, the equivalent in canned tomatoes, tomato juice or tomato purée can be substituted.

AUBERGINES: *bonjon-e-sia*
Aubergines are cheap and plentiful and play an important part in the Afghan diet. Some (not all) have a bitter taste. To get rid of this, peel and slice the aubergines, sprinkle them with salt and leave them on a plate for about half an hour; then rinse them in cold water and pat dry with a clean cloth before use.

ROSE-WATER: *ab-e-gulab*
In the past, in Britain, rose-water was quite often used as a flavouring in cooking. In Afghanistan it is used both for cooking and for medicinal purposes. It lends a lovely delicate flavour to food and is used in many of the desserts and even one of the *pilau* dishes, *norinj pilau*. Always use a wooden spoon when stirring rose-water as metal spoons will leave a metal tang.

ABOUT THE RECIPES

These are based on my own experiences in Afghanistan, or have been given to me by Afghan friends and relatives. Every one has been tested by me at home in England.

I could not include all the recipes for all the Afghan dishes known to me. In making my choice, I have given preference to those which are the most favoured by Afghans and westerners alike, and for which ingredients and utensils are readily available.

I have aimed throughout to give recipes in their authentic form. But some laborious and time-consuming procedures have been changed, and tips for shortcuts incorporated. Often these modifications have come from Afghans living in the west, who have had to make many adjustments and have worked out for themselves how to maintain their own traditions successfully in a different environment. Where appropriate, I have suggested substitute ingredients.

I explained at the beginning of this chapter that Afghan cooks are not accustomed to using exact measures. I give such measures, without which many of the recipes would be puzzling to non-Afghans, but I don't mean them to be taken too literally. Especially with ingredients like salt, pepper, and cooking oil, amounts can be changed to suit individual tastes.

Although Afghans like to eat meat, many of the main dishes can be prepared without it and are suitable for vegetarians. Afghans themselves have had to adapt their diet in this way in times of shortage and hardship.

LANGUAGES

There are two main languages in Afghanistan: Dari, which is closely related to the Farsi (Persian) spoken in Iran, and Pashtu, which is the language of the Pashtuns. My Afghan family and most of my Afghan friends speak Dari, and this is also the language most commonly used in Kabul, so it was the one I learned. I give the names of dishes in a phonetic transcription of Dari, with apologies to language scholars for any inconsistencies.

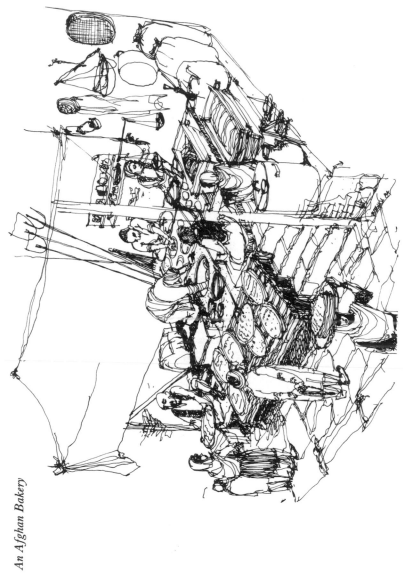

An Afghan Bakery

Bread

Nan, bread and *chai*, tea are the basic diet of all Afghans. The word *nan* actually means food in Afghanistan. The bread is nutritious as well as delicious. The size and shape vary in different parts of the country.

Regular *nan* is made of wholewheat flour and it is leavened with a fermented starter prepared from a small lump of the dough from the previous day. This will have been left in a warm place over-night. It is called *khamir tursh* (sour dough). Most families make their own bread fresh every day and either bake it in their own *tandoor* or take the dough to the local *tandoor* bakery, known as the *nanwaee*. A *tandoor* is a clay oven built into the ground which is capable of reaching temperatures far higher than an ordinary domestic oven. The bread is cooked by flattening the dough against the hot inner wall.

Our family did not have its own *tandoor* so my servant used to prepare the dough first thing in the morning and leave it to rise in a sunny place for an hour or so. Then she would form the dough into round balls of equal size and carry these on her head, balanced on a large tray made from woven straw (*tukri nan*) to the *nanwaee*. The dough would be left there to be baked and she would collect the breads later on, usually in time for lunch. The number of breads baked for us each day would be notched on a long stick called a *chobe khat*. At the end of the week the number of notches were added up so that we could pay our bill. It was of course possible to buy *nan* which was both prepared and baked at the *nanwaee*.

Breads are also baked in Uzbek ovens and on a *tawah*. This is a curved, circular cast iron plate which is heated before the bread is slapped on to it. As the plate is portable this method is especially used by the nomads (*kuchi*) of Afghanistan. The bread cooked on a *tawah* is unleavened and known as *chappatti* or *nan-e-tawagi*.

Lawausha is another popular bread which is similar in size and shape to *chappatti* but is leavened and baked in a *tandoor*.

Uzbek bread differs little from regular *nan* except that it is usually round in shape, a little thicker, and is pricked all over with a fork and glazed with egg before baking. *Nan-e-roghani* and *roht* bread are often served for breakfast or with tea. *Nan-e-roghani* contains a little oil but is basically the same as regular *nan*. *Roht* is a sweet bread containing sugar, milk and fat.

Afghans use finely ground wholewheat flour for most of their bread but the wholewheat flour found in the west is too coarse so I have substituted *chappatti* or *ata* flour, which can be bought at Asian grocers. The closest British equivalent is wheatmeal flour.

The bread dough must be quite soft and the amount of water you use to form it will depend on the type of flour and the humidity of the air. Adjust the quantity of water suggested in the recipe as necessary. Because the dough is soft, the breads need to be patted or rolled out with a fair amount of extra flour.

Bread is eaten with most meals in Afghanistan and with the right hand. It is used to soak up soup, to scoop up food or for eating with rice and kebabs.

NAN
Bread   makes 2 *nan*

Nan is a leavened bread, made with *khamir tursh* (see introduction to bread). Dried yeast gives the necessary leavening, but the flavour is not quite the same. The method of baking in a *tandoor* oven at very high temperatures also contributes to the flavour. *Nan* can, however, be baked satisfactorily in an ordinary oven, if preheated to the highest setting. It is best when eaten straight from the oven, still warm, although it can be served cold. It can be cut into small pieces or served whole. Traditionally, *nan* is served with every meal and eaten without butter. It is, however, also delicious with butter, and perhaps even cheese, or jam.

½ oz (14 g) dried yeast	1 lb (450 g) *chappatti* flour
1 tsp sugar	1 tsp salt
¼ pint (150 ml) warm water	¼ pint (150 ml) cold water

Combine the yeast, sugar and water as directed on the packet of yeast. Leave in a warm place for 10-15 minutes or until the mixture is frothy and the yeast has dissolved.

Sift together the flour and salt and add to the yeast mixture. Gradually, add the water to the flour and yeast and mix with the hand, adding enough water to produce a smooth, round soft dough. Put the dough on to a lightly floured work surface and knead for about 7-10 minutes until it is smooth and essentially the same consistency as ordinary bread dough, then form it into a ball. Put the ball of dough back into the bowl and allow it to stand, covered, in a moderately warm and draught-free place for at least one hour or until the dough has doubled in bulk.

Put in the oven your heaviest and largest baking tray or sheet. You will probably need two baking trays, one for each *nan*. It is also a good idea to line them with heavy aluminium foil. Preheat the oven to the highest temperature.

Divide the dough into two balls and then either roll or shape into oval, flat pieces. Usually *nan* is shaped to about 7″ by 12″ (18 by 30 cm) and ¼″ to ½″ (5 mm to 1 cm) thick. After shaping the *nan*, wet your hand and form deep grooves down the centre of each. In Afghanistan the grooves are made with either fingers and thumb or a cutter and this depends on whether the baker is a woman or a man. Cuts are made by men, grooves by women.

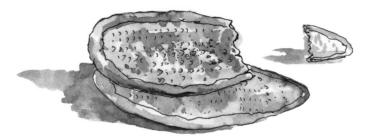

Remove the hot baking trays from the oven and quickly but carefully place a *nan* on each of them. Bake immediately for approximately 8-10 minutes, perhaps a little longer. The dough should be set and the *nan* beginning to brown. The bread should be quite crisp and hard on the outside.

Remove from the baking tray and wrap in a clean tea towel or tin foil until ready for serving.

LAWAUSHA   makes 4 breads

To make *lawausha*, prepare the dough as for *nan*, but roll out to a larger, thinner size. For 1 lb flour you may need to divide the dough into four, rather than two, in order to fit them on to a baking sheet. The cooking time will be slightly less.

NAN-E-UZBEKI   makes 2 breads

To make *nan-e-Uzbeki*, which is a bread found in the north of Afghanistan, prepare the dough as for *nan*, but roll out in a round shape with slightly thicker edges, prick all over with a fork and glaze with egg. Sesame seeds and/or black cumin seeds (*kalonji*) may be sprinkled over the top. The cooking time is slightly longer.

NAN-E-ROGHANI makes 2 breads

Nan-e-roghani is basically *nan*, except that it contains a little oil
and is usually served with tea for breakfast or in the afternoon.
This bread is often brushed with an egg glaze before baking and
sprinkled with black cumin seed or poppy seed.

½ oz (14 g) dried yeast   3-6 tsp vegetable oil
1 tsp sugar   1 tsp salt
¼ pint (150 ml) warm water   4 fl oz (110 ml) water
1 lb (450 g) sifted *chappatti*   egg (for glazing)
    flour   black cumin or poppy seeds

Prepare the dough the same way as for *nan*, adding the oil little
by little. Knead thoroughly. Leave the dough to rise as for *nan*.

Brush oil over the baking tray(s) and preheat the oven to its
highest setting. Divide the dough in two and roll out in the same
way as for *nan*. Prick all over with a fork, glaze with egg and
sprinkle with seeds. Place the *nan* on the baking tray(s). Put into
the oven and cook for about 5 minutes, then reduce the heat to
220°C (425°F, mark 7) and cook for a further 5-10 minutes or
until lightly browned. Then turn the breads over and bake for
yet a further 5-10 minutes, or until the underside is brown.

When you remove the breads from the oven, sprinkle a little
water on both sides, put into a clean cloth and fold over.
Alternatively, wrap the bread in tin foil. This keeps it moist and
soft until ready to eat.

ROHT
Sweet, round flat bread   makes 1 large or 2 small breads

Usually eaten with tea or hot milk at breakfast. It is also made for the festivities when a newborn child is forty days old.

1 lb (450 g) *chappatti* flour
4 oz (110 g) sugar
4 tsp yoghurt (optional)
4 fl oz (110 ml) milk
4 oz (110 g) butter *or*
  margarine

⅛ oz (3½ g) fast acting yeast
1½ tsp baking powder
poppy (or sesame) seed
black cumin seed
1 egg, beaten

Sift the flour into a bowl, add the sugar, yoghurt (if used), milk, melted butter or margarine, the yeast and the baking powder. Then add most of the beaten egg, reserving some for glazing. Mix well and knead for about ten minutes, forming a soft dough. If too sticky, add a little more flour. Leave covered, in a warm place for 1 hour. Roll out the dough to a thickness of about ½″ to ¾″ (1 to 2 cm) and prick all over with a fork. Brush with the remaining beaten egg and sprinkle over the seeds.

Cook on a lightly oiled baking tray in the oven at 250°C (500°F, mark 9) until beginning to brown (5-8 minutes). Reduce the temperature to 120°C (240°F, mark 1¼) and bake until cooked through (check with a fork—about 10-15 minutes). When still warm, place in a plastic bag for about 20 minutes to stop the *roht* drying out too much.

CHAPPATTI
Flat bread   makes 8

Best eaten hot and freshly made. Usually served with kebabs and meat dishes such as *do-piaza*. The ingredients are simple:

chappatti flour : water : salt

Sift 8 oz (225 g) of the flour with ½ tsp salt into a bowl and slowly add water, mixing with the hand, to form a soft dough. About 5 fl oz (150 ml) water should be right. Knead for about 7-10 minutes until the dough is smooth. Cover with a damp cloth and set aside for an hour.

Heat a large cast iron frying-pan (which serves well instead of the traditional *tawah* described on page 43) over a medium heat. Divide the dough into eight and form into round balls. Roll out each ball, using a little extra flour, until it is quite thin and about 7″ to 8″ (18 cm to 20 cm) in diameter. (Afghans usually make larger, oval shapes, but the size recommended fits a frying-pan better.) Pick up each *chappatti* in turn between two hands and pat it gently to shake off excess flour, then slap it on to the hot pan. Cook for about 1 minute, then turn over and cook for about another minute. As you cook, press down the edges gently with tongs, so as to cook evenly. The *chappatti* should puff up. As each is done, put it on a dish, covered with a serviette to keep warm.

KULCHA NAMAKI
Savoury biscuits   makes about 15

1lb plain white or *chappatti* flour	¼ pint (150 ml) milk
1 tsp baking powder	egg yolk for glazing
1 tsp salt	black cumin and sesame seeds
8 oz (225 g) margarine	aniseed for sprinkling

Sift the flour, baking powder and salt into a bowl and then rub in the margarine until the mixture resembles bread crumbs. Add the milk gradually and mix gently to form a dough. Leave to stand for half an hour.

Form a piece of the dough into a size and shape slightly larger than a ping pong ball. Roll out on a lightly floured board to a thickness of ⅛″ (3 mm). Repeat with all the dough. (Alternatively, the dough can be rolled out and the biscuits cut out with a pastry cutter.) Prick the biscuits all over with a fork, then brush with beaten egg yolk. Sprinkle with the seeds.

Bake the biscuits on a greased baking tray(s) in an oven preheated to 200°C (400°F, mark 6) until golden brown for approximately 15-20 minutes.

These biscuits are often eaten at tea time, along with sweet ones.

Soups, Pasta, and Snacks

Soup, *sherwa*, is one of the basic foods, especially among the poorer people. The usual way is to break up bread into the soup to soak and then to eat it either with the hand or with a spoon.

These soups are very filling and nourishing and so they are often prepared as a main meal. *Sherwa-e-tarkori* is perhaps the most common, made with meat and vegetables, but the ingredients vary according to what is available. It is quite usual for fresh coriander to be added as it lends such a delicious flavour to the soup. Other soups include *sherwa birinj*, a rice soup; *maushawa*, a pulse and yoghurt soup; and *aush*, a pasta soup with yoghurt.

Various pasta dishes are popular. There are many theories about their origins, but it is agreed that they do come from somewhere along the Silk Route from the Far East to Italy. Many Afghan pasta dishes are similar to Italian ones. For example, *ashak* closely resembles ravioli and *lakhchak* is very similar to lasagne. *Mantu*, an Uzbek dish rather like a steamed meat dumpling, is included here; it probably comes from Tibet.

Snacks include *boulanee*, a traditional fried pastry filled with *gandana* (Chinese chives, p 40) or with mashed potato.

SHERWA-E-TARKORI
Meat and vegetable soup   serves 4

This soup is very common and there are no hard and fast rules. There are many versions and ingredients vary according to what vegetables are available. Lamb, beef or chicken may be used for the meat.

3 fl oz (75 ml) vegetable oil	1½-2 pints (about 1 litre) water
2 medium onions, chopped	
1 lb (450 g) meat on the bone cut into small pieces	8 oz (225 g) potatoes ⎱ peeled 4 oz (110 g) carrots ⎰ & cubed
1 small can tomatoes (227 g)	2 oz (50 g) fresh coriander salt and pepper

Heat the oil in a large pan and fry the onions over a medium to high heat until golden brown and soft. Add the meat and continue frying until the meat is brown all over. Add the tomatoes, salt, pepper and the water. Bring to the boil, then turn down the heat and simmer for a further 20-30 minutes or until the vegetables are cooked. Wash the coriander and remove the stalks and then add to the soup. Cook for a further 5 minutes or so, adding a little more water if required.

This soup is always served with a fresh *nan* or *chappatti*.

SHERWA-E-SHAMALI-WAR

'Hot' meat and vegetable soup   serves 6

This soup comes from the north of Kabul; its name translates to mean 'soup of the northerners'. It is renowned for its hot and spicy flavour.

¼ pint (150 ml) vegetable oil	1 or 2 hot red or green peppers
10 oz (275 g) onions, sliced thinly	2 tsp ground coriander
	1-2 tsp turmeric
2 cloves of garlic, peeled and crushed	1-2 tsp black pepper, ground
	3½ pints (2 litres) water
1½ lb (700 g) meat on the bone, preferably lamb	1 lb (450 g) potatoes, peeled and cut into cubes if large
2 oz (50 g) split peas	4 oz (110 g) fresh coriander
1 lb (450 g) tomatoes skinned and roughly chopped	salt

Heat the oil in a large pan and fry the onions over a medium to high heat until golden brown and soft. Add the garlic and the meat and continue frying until the meat is brown all over. Add the split peas, tomatoes, peppers and spices and then the water. Bring to the boil, turn down the heat and simmer until the meat is almost cooked. Then add the potatoes and fresh coriander, which first should have had the stalks removed, and simmer for a further 20-30 minutes or until the potatoes are soft. If the liquid has reduced too much, add extra water. Add salt.

This soup is served with fresh *nan* or *chappatti* with a side dish of sliced onions marinated in vinegar, or a mixed salad.

SHERWA BIRINJ
Rice soup   serves 4

An economical and simple soup, for which the recipe is flexible. The lamb or chicken may be left-overs, and Afghans might use meatballs instead of meat. The amount of vegetables can be adjusted as you please.

3 oz (75 g) short grain rice	1 tbs powdered dill
2 pints (1.1 litre) water	1 tomato, chopped
2 fl oz (55 ml) vegetable oil	1 medium potato ⎱ peeled
2-4 oz (50-75 g) lamb or	1 medium carrot ⎰ & cubed
chicken, cut into small	salt and pepper, to taste
pieces	

Wash the rice and put in a large pan and cover with about 2 pints of water. Add the oil, meat, dill, vegetables and salt and pepper. Bring to the boil, cover with a lid, leaving it slightly ajar, then turn down the heat and simmer until the rice is soft and the meat and vegetables cooked, stirring from time to time.

SHERWA-E-LAHWANG
Yoghurt soup with tomatoes   serves 3-4

I first tasted this recipe at the home of my friend, Mrs Parwin Ali. It comes from the south-east area of Afghanistan. She has kindly sent me her recipe and I find it easy to make.

15 fl oz (425 ml) yoghurt	½ pint (275 ml) water
2 cloves of garlic, peeled and	2 tbs plain flour
crushed	½ tsp turmeric
2 oz (50 g) margarine	salt
3 medium tomatoes, skinned	
and chopped	

Strain the yoghurt for about one hour so that it becomes *chaka* (p 38), or buy ready strained yoghurt.

Fry the garlic in the margarine until brown. Add the tomatoes and stir and fry until reddish-brown.

Blend the *chaka*, water, flour, turmeric and salt, either by hand or in a mixer. Then slowly add to the garlic and tomatoes. Bring to the boil, turn the heat down and simmer until the soup is thickened.

SHERWA-E-PIAWA
Potato soup   serves 4

In Afghanistan this is a poor man's soup and is usually made in winter.

1 lb (450 g) potatoes, peeled and cut into 1" (2.5 cm) cubes	1½-2 pints (about 1 litre) water
3 fl oz (75 ml) vegetable oil	1 tsp turmeric
2 medium onions, chopped	salt and red pepper, to taste

Heat the oil in a pan and fry the onions over a medium to high heat until nearly brown. Add the potatoes. Stir and fry until the potatoes are well coated with the oil. Add the water, turmeric and salt and red pepper to taste. Simmer until the potatoes are cooked.

Serve with fresh *nan*.

MAUSHAWA
Pulse and yoghurt soup   serves 4-6

In Afghanistan this soup is served either as a starter or as a main meal. This is the original version of *maushawa*, cooked with meat *qorma* but another popular version is made using meatballs (*kofta*). The meatballs are prepared as for the *kofta* in *kofta chalau*, but are smaller (about ½" or 1 cm in diameter). The sauce remains the same too, except that the yoghurt should be omitted. Afghans like to serve this soup 'hot', but seasoning can be adjusted according to taste.

2 oz (50 g) chickpeas	*for the meat stew*
2 oz (50 g) red kidney beans	8 oz (225 g) beef, veal or lamb
15 fl oz (425 ml) yoghurt	cut in ½" (1 cm) cubes
2 oz (50 g) mung beans	4 oz (110 g) finely chopped
(or green split peas)	onion
2 oz (50 g) short grain rice	3 tbs vegetable oil
2 pints (about 1 litre) water	2 oz (50 g) tomatoes, skinned
including the water for	and chopped
soaking the pulses	¼ pint (150 ml) water
2 tsp powdered dill	¼-1 tsp red pepper
salt	salt

Soak the chick peas and red kidney beans in water overnight. Drain the yoghurt for about an hour to make *chaka* (p 38). Put the chickpeas, red kidney beans, mung beans (or green split peas) and rice in a large pan with the 2 pints of water, including the water in which the pulses have been soaked. Bring to the boil, cover leaving the lid slightly ajar, turn the heat to low and simmer. Cook until the pulses are soft (the time this takes depends on the freshness of the pulses).

Meanwhile cook the meat and sauce. Heat the vegetable oil in a pan and add the chopped onion. Fry over a medium heat until soft and reddish-brown. Add the meat and fry again until brown. Add the tomatoes, stirring well and boil for a minute or so. Add the ¼ pint of water, the salt and red pepper. Stir well and bring back to the boil. Turn down the heat and simmer until the meat is tender and the sauce thickened.

When cooked, mix all the ingredients; the rice, chickpeas, red kidney beans, together with the juices in which they have cooked, the meat stew, the *chaka*, powdered dill and salt to taste. Stir well and add extra water if you want to thin the soup. Continue stirring and simmer for another 5-10 minutes to allow the flavours to blend.

Serve the *maushawa* hot in individual soup plates or cups. *Nan* is usually served with this soup.

AUSH-E-ASLI
Pasta, yoghurt and meatballs   serves 4

Aush is one of the well known and popular dishes. It is very versatile and families have their own variations. Afghans often prepare it to cure colds and then they add plenty of garlic and lots of red pepper as they say it helps clear the head and chest. It is filling and is usually eaten as a main course, but smaller quantities can be served as a first course. This recipe is for the original *aush*, known as *aush-e-asli*.

Afghans usually make their own spaghetti or noodles from the same dough used for *boulanee* (p 66). The dough is rolled out very thinly to ⅟₁₆″ (1½ mm), then rolled up tightly and cut into fine strips with a sharp knife. The spaghetti is then tossed in a little flour and allowed to dry on a board. The spaghetti can be cooked straight away or stored in a covered jar for a couple of days. I have used fresh spaghetti, noodles or tagliatelle in this recipe as it saves time and fresh pasta is now available at many delicatessens and supermarkets.

15 fl oz (425 ml) yoghurt
8 oz (225 g) fresh spaghetti or
    tagliatelle
1¾ pints (1 litre) water, well
    salted

¼-½ tsp red pepper
2-3 cloves of garlic, peeled and
    crushed
1 tbs dried mint

for the meatballs
1 lb (450 g) minced beef or
    lamb
1 medium onion, minced or
    grated
1 tsp ground coriander
1 tsp ground cumin
½ tsp ground black pepper
1 egg (optional)
salt

for the sauce
3 fl oz (75 ml) vegetable oil
2 medium onions, finely
    chopped
4 oz (110 g) tomatoes, peeled
    and chopped (optional)
3 fl oz (75 ml) water
salt and pepper

Drain the yoghurt for about an hour to make *chaka* (p 38), or buy ready strained yoghurt.

Prepare the meatballs. Combine the minced meat, onions,

spices, egg and salt and mix thoroughly. Knead until smooth and form into small balls about ½" (1 cm) in diameter.

Prepare the sauce. Heat the vegetable oil in a pan and add the onions. Fry, stirring continuously over a medium to high heat until soft and reddish-brown. Add the tomatoes, if used, and stir and fry briskly until the sauce turns brownish. Add the water, salt and pepper and bring back to simmering point. Add the meatballs, one at a time, in a single layer, then cover, leaving the lid slightly ajar, turn down the heat to low and simmer gently for about half an hour, or until the meatballs and sauce have a browned look and the sauce has thickened. If the sauce is too thick you can add a little water.

To cook the *aush*, put about 1½-1¾ pints (1 litre) of water into a large pan and bring to the boil. Add plenty of salt and the spaghetti; bring back to the boil, then turn down the heat to medium and cook uncovered and gently for 10-15 minutes. Do not drain. Then add the meatballs and sauce, the *chaka*, red pepper and the mint. Mix and stir well. Turn down the heat to low and leave to simmer slowly for about 10 minutes to let the flavours blend.

Meanwhile, fry the crushed garlic in a little oil and add to the *aush*, then serve, hot. Some Afghans like it very thick, others prefer a thinner soup and add extra water.

This dish can be prepared in advance and reheated.

AUSH
Pasta with yoghurt, chickpeas, kidney beans and minced meat   serves 4-6

Another version of *aush* which is also delicious. The recipe includes chickpeas and red kidney beans and, instead of the meatballs, minced meat is served separately and added on top of the *aush*.

2 oz (50 g) chick peas
2 oz (50 g) red kidney beans
15 fl oz (425 ml) yoghurt
2 pints (about 1 litre) water
8 oz (225 g) fresh spaghetti
   or tagliatelle
salt
red pepper, according to taste
1 tbs dried mint

for the minced meat
3 fl oz (75 ml) vegetable oil
2 medium onions, finely
   chopped
1 lb (450 g) minced beef or
   lamb
¼ pint (150 ml) water (or
   tomato juice)
1 tsp ground coriander
salt and pepper

Soak the peas and beans in water overnight.

Drain the yoghurt for about 1 hour to make *chaka* (p 38), or buy ready strained yoghurt.

Put the chick peas and red kidney beans into a large pan with the water in which they were soaked and add ¼ pint (150 ml) of water. Bring to the boil, then reduce the heat and boil gently until cooked, adding extra water if necessary. Cooking time will vary according to the freshness of the pulses.

While the pulses are cooking, prepare the meat. Heat the oil in a pan over a medium to high heat. Add the chopped onions and fry, stirring continuously until they are reddish-brown. Add the meat and stir well. Fry until brown. Add the water (or tomatoes) and bring to the boil. Add the coriander, salt and pepper to taste. Stir again, then turn down the heat and simmer for about half an hour or until the meat is cooked. Add extra water if the mixture becomes too dry.

When the meat and pulses are cooked, bring to the boil 1½-1¾ pints of water in a large pan. Add salt and the spaghetti or tagliatelle, and boil gently for about 10-15 minutes. Add the peas, beans, *chaka*, and some or all of the juices from the peas and beans, depending on how thick you want the soup. Add the dried mint, salt and red pepper and mix well. More water can be added if required. Leave on a low heat for about 10 minutes or so to let the flavours blend. Serve the soup and top with a little of the meat. The remaining meat is served separately and later added to the top of each individual portion of *aush*.

This dish can be prepared in advance and reheated.

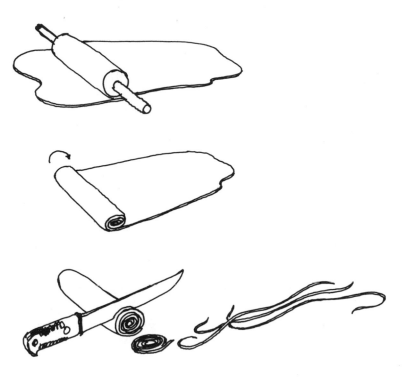

ASHAK

Leek-filled pasta with meat sauce   serves 4, or 8 as a first course

This delicious and famous pasta dish requires time and patience but the effort is well worth it. In Afghanistan, the filling is *gandana* (Chinese chives, p 40) but leeks make a good substitute. It is usually served with minced meat and *chaka*.

1 lb (450 g) plain white flour	1 tsp vinegar
4 tsp salt	1 tbs ground mint
1 egg	
2 tbs vegetable oil	*for the meat sauce:*
¼ pint (150 ml) water	3 fl oz (85 ml) vegetable oil
1 lb (450 g) finely chopped	1-2 medium onions, finely
leeks	chopped
½ tsp red pepper	1 lb (450 g) minced beef or
15 fl oz (425 ml) yoghurt	lamb
3½ pints (2 litres) water	¼ pint (150 ml) tomato
3 cloves garlic, peeled and	juice or water
crushed	salt and black pepper

Prepare the dough. Sift the flour and 1 teaspoon of salt into a large mixing bowl, make a well and add the egg and 1 tablespoon of oil. Add the water slowly and knead thoroughly to form a smooth dough. Divide the dough into two balls and cover with a damp cloth for about an hour.

Wash the leeks, squeeze hard to drain, and place in a colander. Add 1 teaspoon of salt and the red pepper. Knead until the leeks begin to soften and then mix in the other tablespoon of oil.

Drain the yoghurt for 1 hour to make *chaka* (p 38).

Roll out one ball of the dough on to a lightly floured surface to a thickness of ⅟₁₆″ (1½ mm—no thicker, or the *ashak* will be tough). Cut out rounds (2½″ or 6 cm diameter) with a cutter. Put 1-2 teaspoons of the drained leeks on half of the rounds. Use the other half to cover the leeks and seal the edges carefully. Place the prepared *ashak* on to a well floured sheet or tray. Do not place on top of each other as they will stick together. Repeat with the remaining dough.

Place the *chaka* in a bowl and mix in the garlic and 1 teaspoon of salt. Put half of the *chaka* on a flat dish in a warm place.

Bring the water to the boil in a large pan and add the vinegar and 1 teaspoon of salt. Drop in the *ashak* and boil gently for about 10 minutes, pushing them down carefully with a slotted spoon as they rise to the surface. When cooked, remove with a large slotted spoon or sieve taking care not to break them. Drain thoroughly and place the *ashak* on to the dish on top of the *chaka*. Cover with the remaining *chaka* and sprinkle over the mint. Top with a little of the minced meat and serve at once together with a separate bowl of meat.

TO PREPARE THE MEAT SAUCE. Heat the oil in a pan, add the onions and fry, stirring continuously, until they are reddish-brown. Add the meat, stir and fry until brown. Mix in the tomato juice or water and bring to the boil. Add salt and black pepper. Stir well, then lower the heat and simmer until the sauce is thick and oily (½-1 hour). Afghans like it oily, but some of the oil can be spooned off.

MANTU
Pasta filled with meat and onion   serves 4, or 8 as a first course

This most traditional of all Uzbek dishes is probably of Tibetan origin. I spent a very enjoyable day with the Rashidzada family, who kindly showed me how to make *mantu*. It is very tasty but does require some preparation. Uzbeks usually serve *mantu* as an appetizer and then follow it with a *pilau*, such as *qabili pilau Uzbeki*. You will need a large steamer for this recipe. Some people use minced meat to save time, but it works less well as the meat tends to form a hard lump inside the pasta.

15 fl oz (425 ml) yoghurt
1 lb (450 g) plain white flour
2-3 tsp salt
7-8 fl oz (225 ml) water
1 lb (450 g) boneless fatty
    lamb, chopped into very
    small pieces
1 lb (450 g) onions, finely
    chopped

1 green chilli pepper, finely
    chopped (optional)
1-2 tsp ground black pepper
1-2 tsp ground cumin
1 tbs vegetable oil
1 tbs tomato purée
1 tbs fresh coriander, finely
    chopped

Drain the yoghurt for about an hour to make *chaka* (p 38), or buy ready strained yoghurt.
    Prepare the dough. Sift the flour with about 1 teaspoon salt into a mixing bowl. Add, slowly, as much water as required and mix to form a stiff dough. Place the dough on a clean work surface and knead for 5-10 minutes or until the dough is elastic and shiny. Form the dough into a ball, cover with a damp cloth and set aside, for about an hour.
    Put the chopped lamb, onions, chilli, salt, pepper and spices in a bowl and mix thoroughly.
    Divide the dough into four small balls which will make it easier to roll out. Roll out to a thickness of about 1/16" (1½ mm) on a lightly floured surface. Cut into 4" (10 cm) squares. Into each square put about 1 heaped tablespoon of meat mixture. Take two opposite corners and bring them to join in the centre by nipping together firmly between your fingers. Nip together the two remaining corners as shown in the diagram on the next

page. The *mantu* should not be sealed completely as the steam has to be able to penetrate and cook the filling. The method of sealing them varies but I have found this way to be the simplest. Use fat to grease well the shelves of the steamer. This prevents the *mantu* from sticking. Place them on the shelves leaving a small space between each one. Steam for 30-45 minutes over a medium heat.

While the *mantu* are steaming, make the tomato sauce. Heat the oil in a pan, add the tomato purée and bring to the boil. Turn down the heat, stir and simmer until the *mantu* are ready.

Remove the *mantu* carefully from the steam shelves and place on a large, warm dish. Spoon the tomato sauce over the top and sprinkle with the chopped coriander. Serve the *chaka* in a separate bowl.

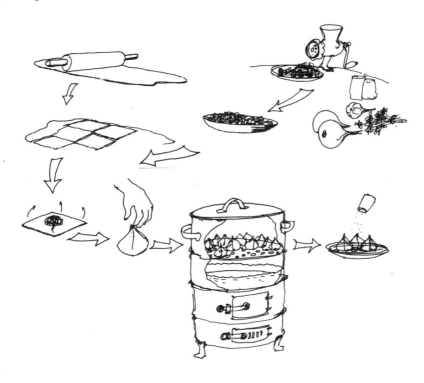

LAKHCHAK
Afghan lasagne serves 4 to 6

Lakhchak is similar to Italian lasagne. It is simple to make, especially if you buy ready-made fresh lasagne. Alternatively, make the same dough as for *ashak* (p 60) or for *boulanee* (p 66).

for the meat sauce
3 fl oz (75 ml) vegetable oil
2 medium onions, chopped
1 lb (450 g) minced beef or
  lamb
¼ pint (150 ml) water or
  tomato juice
1 tsp ground coriander
salt and pepper

for the lakhchak
15 fl oz (425 ml) yoghurt
2-3 cloves of garlic, peeled
  and crushed
salt
1 lb (450 g) fresh *lakhchak* or
  lasagne
1-2 tbs olive oil or corn oil
1 tbs dried mint

Cook the meat as in the recipe for *aush* (p 58).

Drain the yoghurt for about 1 hour to make *chaka* (p 38). Add the peeled and crushed garlic and a little salt to the *chaka*.

Cut the *lakhchak* into 2″ (5 cm) squares, or into any shape you wish. (Do not make the shapes too big or they will be difficult to handle.) If you are making your own homemade dough, roll it out thinly, to about ¹⁄₁₆″ (1½ mm) and cut into shapes.

Boil plenty of salted water in a large pan and add 1-2 tablespoons of oil. (This helps prevent the *lakhchak* sticking together.) Add the *lakhchak* one at a time to the boiling water and cook for 10-12 minutes. If you cannot cook the *lakhchak* all in one go, cook half and keep them warm while cooking the second batch.

Spoon about one third of the *chaka* on to a large, warm dish, then add half of the cooked *lakhchak*. Spoon another third of the *chaka* over the top and cover with half of the meat sauce. Sprinkle with a little of the mint. Add the rest of the *lakhchak*, cover with the remaining *chaka* and remaining meat sauce. Sprinkle with the remaining mint. Serve immediately.

VARIATION. Some Afghans fry chopped Chinese chives (p 40, but you can use leeks) in a little oil and put them between the *lakhchak*. ½-1 lb (225-450 g) of leeks are enough.

PAKAURA
Deep fried potatoes in batter   serves 4

These make a tasty snack and are usually served with chutney.

4 oz (110 g) *chapatti* or wheatmeal flour	¼ tsp saffron or turmeric
1 egg	¼ tsp red pepper
¼ pint (150 ml) water	4 medium to large potatoes (about 1½ lb (700 g))
salt	vegetable oil for deep-frying

Make a batter using the flour, eggs and water and add a pinch of salt. Beat well and then set to one side for half an hour or so. Add the saffron or turmeric and red pepper.

Scrub the potatoes and boil in their skins for 8-10 minutes. Leave to cool and then slice into rounds about ¼" (5 mm) thick.

Heat the vegetable oil in a deep frying-pan until very hot, then dip the potato slices in the batter, coating well on both sides. Put into the hot oil to deep fry. Fry several at a time. They will rise to the surface and when they are golden brown, remove them from the oil and drain. Sprinkle with extra salt and pepper and serve hot with chutney.

65

BOULANEE
Leek filled pastries   makes approximately 15

These used to be a great favourite among foreigners in Afghanistan and are delicious especially when served with drinks. They should be served crisp and hot, straight from the frying-pan. However, Afghans occasionally serve them cold, especially if there are a lot of other dishes being served at the same time. They are made on special occasions such as birthdays and engagements, but can also be served as snacks.

Two types of *boulanee* are prepared in Afghanistan. The most popular is that made with *gandana* (Chinese chives, p 40) but leeks make a good substitute. *Boulanee* are also made with a mashed potato filling. I have given the recipe for this next. Often at parties or special occasions both types of *boulanee* are prepared at the same time.

1 lb (450 g) sifted white plain flour (or half white, half *chappatti*)	3 tsp salt
	½ tsp red pepper
	1 tbs vegetable oil
7-8 fl oz (225 ml) water	plus extra for frying
1 lb (450 g) Chinese chives or leeks (trimmed weight), washed and finely chopped	

Put the flour and 1 teaspoon of salt into a mixing bowl. Add slowly as much water as required and mix to form a stiff dough. Place the dough on to a clean work surface and knead for about 5-10 minutes until the dough is elastic, smooth and shiny. Form the dough into a ball, cover with a damp cloth and set aside for at least half an hour.

Squeeze out as much water as possible from the leeks and put into a colander. Add 1-2 teaspoons salt and ½ teaspoon red pepper. Mix and knead by hand until the leeks begin to soften and then add 1 tablespoon of oil. Mix again before setting aside.

Divide the dough into three or four balls. Roll out each ball as thinly as possible on a lightly floured surface (the thickness should be no more than ¹⁄₁₆″ (1½ mm)—if the dough is too thick the *boulanee* will be tough). Take a round cutter of 5-6 inches (13-15 cm), (a pan lid or tin lid can be used) and cut out as many rounds as possible. The number of *boulanee* will depend on how thinly the dough is rolled out and the size of cutter used. On half of each round spread about 2-3 tablespoons of the drained leeks. Moisten the edges of the dough, fold over and seal shut. The *boulanee* should be spread out on a lightly floured surface until ready to fry. Do not place one *boulanee* on top of another as they will stick together.

When all the *boulanee* are made and you are ready to serve them, heat enough vegetable oil in a frying-pan and shallow fry one or two *boulanee* at a time, browning on both sides. Keep warm until all are finished. Serve at once.

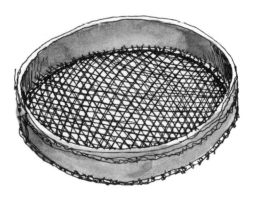

A typical Afghan sieve used to produce finer wholemeal flour needed in the preparation of Boulanee

BOULANEE KATCHALU
Boulanee *with a potato filling*   makes approximately 15

1 lb (450 g) sifted white plain flour (or half white, half *chappatti*)	2 lb (900 g) potatoes
	2 oz (50 g) spring onions, finely chopped
7-8 fl oz (225 ml) water	1 tsp black pepper
3 tsp salt	vegetable oil for frying

Make the dough as for the *boulanee* filled with leeks (p 66).

Peel and wash the potatoes and boil them in salted water until soft. Drain off the water and mash thoroughly. Add the spring onions, salt and black pepper.

Roll out the dough as for the *boulanee* with leeks and cut out as many rounds as possible. On half of each round spread 1-2 tablespoons of the mashed potatoes. Moisten the edges of the dough, fold over and seal shut.

Continue as for the *boulanee* with leeks.

SAMBOSA GOSHTI
Fried pastries filled with minced meat   makes approximately 24

Sambosa are another popular snack and ideal for serving with drinks. They are similar to the Indian *samosa* but are not so hot and spicy. If preferred frozen puff pastry can be used instead of the pastry given below. Some Afghans use the same pastry as for *ashak*.

1 lb (450 g) plain white flour	7-8 fl oz (225 ml) water
salt	6 tbs oil (approximately)

for the filling

1 lb (450 g) minced meat	1 tsp ground cumin
4 oz (110 g) onion, finely chopped	1 tsp ground coriander
	1 tsp black pepper
2 tbs vegetable oil	salt
	vegetable oil for frying

Sift the flour into a bowl with about ½ teaspoon salt. Add slowly as much water as required, mixing to form a stiff dough.

Knead for a few minutes until smooth. Form into seven equal balls. Cover with a damp cloth and leave for 15-30 minutes.

To prepare the filling; put the meat and chopped onion in a pan with the 2 tablespoons of vegetable oil and fry gently for about 15-30 minutes. Add the cumin, coriander, black pepper and salt. Cook for a few more minutes, stirring well. Drain off the excess oil and juices.

Roll out each ball of dough into paper thinness on a lightly floured board. Brush six layers with about 1 tablespoon of oil each. Place the layers on top of each other, ending with the seventh layer. Roll out again thinly, trying not to stretch the pastry too much. Cut into 4″ (10 cm) squares. As with *boulanee*, the number of *sambosa* will vary according to how thinly the dough is rolled out.

Inside each square, spoon about 1 tablespoon of the cooked meat. Fold the filled pastry into a triangle and seal shut tightly. Repeat until all the squares are filled.

Heat enough vegetable oil in a pan to deep fry the *sambosa* until golden brown on both sides. Remove from the oil and drain.

Sambosa are served hot or cold, but personally I think they are tastier if served hot.

KABABI

TSCHARIKARI

A kebab stall

Kebabs

In every town and city of Afghanistan there are numerous kebab stalls or restaurants and often, while walking round the bazaars, I would find myself drawn to them by the sound of eastern music and the smell of kebabs cooking over charcoal. The stallholder stood over or sat near the kebabs, wafting his *pakka* (kebab fan) over them to keep the charcoals glowing. (The charcoal burners are ventilated metal boxes about 5″ wide, 4″ deep and 2-3′ long.)

Kebabs are usually made with lamb, either cubed, on the bone or minced, and are cooked by grilling over charcoal on kebab skewers called *sikh*. Some types of kebabs are fried, and some are baked in a *tandoor* or other oven. *Chappatti*, or sometimes *nan*, are served with the kebabs, along with sliced onions and tomatoes or perhaps a salad. For added flavour they are sprinkled with crushed grape seeds and red pepper. Kebabs are usually followed by plenty of sweet green tea with cardamom, as this helps the digestion.

I have included in this section two dishes which are not really kebabs but meat dishes served with bread rather than rice. They are *do piaza*, a lamb dish cooked with onions and split peas and *qorma rui nan*, a meat dish served with fried bread, *chaka* and leeks.

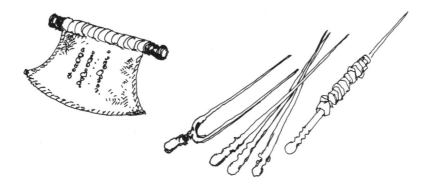

SIKH OR TIKKA KEBAB
Lamb kebab   serves 4-6

Of all kebabs these are the most favoured by Afghans and are the best known. The kebabs are traditionally cooked over a charcoal fire. Use a barbecue if you have one. Otherwise, an electric oven or gas grill is satisfactory, although of course the flavour will not be the same. The lamb is threaded on to kebab skewers (*sikh*). If using an ordinary grill, balance the skewers on the rim of the grill pan in such a way that all the meat juices drip inside the tray.

Sikh kebabs are always served with bread of some kind, usually *chappatti* or *lawausha*, and crushed grape seeds and red pepper are sprinkled on the top for added flavour.

2 lb (900 g) boneless lamb,	salt and black or red pepper
cut into ¾" (2 cm) cubes	2 *lawausha* or *chappatti* (or *nan*)
8 oz (225 g) lamb fat (optional)	
½ pint (275 ml) yoghurt	*for the garnish*
3 tbs lemon juice	onion
4 cloves of garlic,	tomato
peeled and crushed	lemon or lime wedges

Mix the yoghurt, lemon juice, crushed garlic, salt and pepper in a bowl. Add the lamb and lamb fat (if used). Mix well and marinate, covered, in the refrigerator for 6-24 hours.

Preheat the grill. Thread the meat on to the skewers. (The cubes of meat should be alternated with the fat, if used.) Grill, turning frequently, for about 15-20 minutes until brown and cooked.

Place the *chappatti* or *lawausha* on a large dish, remove the kebabs from the skewers and place them on the bread. Sprinkle with a little salt and pepper, garnish with the tomato, onion and lemon, and fold the *chappatti* or *lawausha* over to keep the kebabs warm. The extra *lawausha* or *chappatti* is cut into pieces and served separately. A salad is a good accompaniment.

KOFTA KEBAB or QIMA KEBAB
Minced meat kebabs   serves 4-6

Cooked in the same way as *sikh kebab*, this kebab is made with
minced meat.

2 lb (900 g) best minced beef | salt and black or red pepper
  or lamb | 2 *lawausha* or *chappatti*
4 oz (110 g) onions | *For the garnish*
3 cloves of garlic, | fresh mint or coriander
  peeled and crushed | lemon wedges

Mince the onions and mix thoroughly with the garlic and meat,
adding salt and pepper. Continue mixing well with the hand
until the mixture becomes sticky. Then wet your hand with
water and mould the mixture round kebab skewers to form
kebabs about 4″ (10 cm) long and 1″ (2.5 cm) in diameter. Press
onto the skewers firmly so that they will hold. Smooth the
kebabs carefully with your wet hand.

Preheat the grill. Grill the kebabs under a high heat. When
they are brown on both sides, reduce the heat to medium and
grill, turning frequently, for about 15 minutes more.

Remove carefully from the skewers and serve on one of the
breads. Sprinkle with a little salt and black or red pepper.
Garnish with fresh mint or coriander and lemon wedges. Fold
the bread over to keep the kebabs warm. The remaining bread,
cut into pieces, is served with them.

SHINWARI KEBAB
Lamb chops kebab   serves 4

Shinwari is the name of one of the large Pashtun tribes of the North West Frontier. This kebab was one of our favourites and we used to invite our friends to the old town of Kabul, by the river, to go and eat it at one of the kebab stalls there. It is extremely simple to prepare.

12-16 best end neck lamb chops, cut thinly salt and black or red pepper *nan* or *chappatti*	*for the garnish* tomato onion lemon

Rub the chops all over but lightly with salt. Leave in a cool place for 15-30 minutes.

Put the chops on to kebab skewers and either cook over charcoal or under a preheated grill for about 20 minutes, turning the kebabs frequently, until brown and cooked.

Remove from the skewers, sprinkle with plenty of pepper and serve on fresh *nan* or *chappatti*. Garnish with tomato, onion and lemon.

QARAYI KEBAB
Lamb kebab with eggs   serves 4

This kebab is prepared individually in round metal pans called *qarayi* which are similar to those used for cooking and serving lasagne or cannelloni in restaurants in Europe. It can, however, be made quite satisfactorily in a frying-pan.

1-1½ lb (450-700 g) boneless
   lamb with fat, cut into ¾"
   (2cm) cubes
¼ pint (150 ml) yoghurt
1-2 tbs lemon juice
	2 cloves of garlic, peeled and
	   crushed
	salt and black or red pepper
	4-8 eggs
	vegetable oil for frying

Prepare and cook the meat as for *sikh kebab* (p 72).

When the kebabs are cooked, remove from the skewers and heat the vegetable oil in a large frying-pan. Add the kebabs and fry quickly for a few seconds, then break the eggs over the top of the meat and fry until the eggs are cooked. Do not stir the eggs or break them. Sprinkle with salt and pepper and serve straight from the pan, with freshly baked *nan* and a salad.

VARIATIONS. Some Afghans fry sliced onions until soft and then add the kebab. This kebab can also be made with meatballs (*kofta*).

SHAMI KEBAB or LOLA KEBAB

A sausage-shaped kebab   makes about 25

These are extremely tasty and ideal for a buffet party as they can be prepared in advance and served either cold or warmed up again in the oven.

2 lb (900 g) boneless lamb, including fat	1 hot green pepper, finely chopped and seeds removed
3 medium onions, quartered	2 cloves of garlic, peeled and and crushed
2 oz (50 g) split peas	4 tsp ground coriander
8 fl oz (225 ml) water	2 eggs
1 lb (450 g) potatoes	salt and pepper
1 sweet red or green pepper, finely chopped	vegetable oil for frying

Boil the meat, onions and split peas in the water until the meat is tender and the split peas soft.

Peel and boil the potatoes separately until soft, then drain well.

Mince the meat, potatoes, onions, two kinds of pepper and crushed garlic together. Add the coriander, eggs, salt and pepper and mix well. The mixture should be soft but firm and not too runny. Add some or all of the remaining stock if it is firm enough, but if it is a little 'sloppy', add up to 4 oz (110 g) flour. With portions of the mixture, form sausage-shaped kebabs, each about 4″ (10 cm) long and 1″ (2.5 cm) in diameter.

Deep fry the kebabs in hot oil, over a medium to high heat, turning carefully until all sides are golden brown and the kebabs are cooked through.

Serve with fresh *nan* or *chappatti* and garnish with fresh mint, coriander or parsley, tomatoes, spring onions and lemon slices or wedges.

CHAPPLI KEBAB
A 'hot' kebab   makes 12

Chappli means sandal in Dari and this kebab is shaped like the sole of a sandal. It comes from the Jalalabad region and is probably derived from the hotter dishes of the Indian subcontinent.

1 lb (450 g) best minced beef or lamb	½ hot green pepper, finely chopped
12 oz (350 g) spring onions, finely chopped	3-4 tbs fresh coriander finely chopped
4 oz (110 g) plain white flour	2 tsp ground coriander
½ sweet pepper, green or red, finely chopped	salt
	vegetable oil for frying

Put the meat, spring onion, flour, both kinds of pepper, fresh and ground coriander in a bowl and mix thoroughly, adding salt to taste. Shape the mixture into flat oblongs about 6″ by 4″ and ¼″ thick (15 cm by 10 cm by 5 mm).

Heat enough vegetable oil in a frying-pan to fry the kebabs (which should be almost covered by the oil), and fry over a medium to high heat until they are brown on both sides and cooked through (about 10 minutes).

Serve with a tomato and onion salad and *chappatti* or *nan*. Garnish with fresh coriander and lemon.

KEBAB-E-DAYGI
Kebab cooked in a pan   serves 4

A recipe given to me by Mrs Parwin Ali, who used to cook this kebab for us at her home. It is simple to prepare.

2 lb (900 g) lamb on the bone	salt
¼ pint (150 ml) yoghurt	1 tsp ground coriander
2 cloves of garlic, peeled and crushed	8 oz (225 g) onions, finely sliced

Cut the meat into serving-sized pieces, and then marinate in the yoghurt, garlic, salt and coriander mixed together. Leave for at least a couple of hours.

Put the meat and yoghurt mixture in a pan and cook gently until the meat is just tender. When it is tender, add the sliced onions and cook further over a medium to low heat until the sauce thickens, the onions have become very soft and the fat from the meat has separated. Stir frequently. Serve with *nan* or *chappatti*, or with plain boiled potatoes.

KEBAB-E-DOSHI
'Oven kebab'   serves 4-6

Kebab-e-doshi means 'oven kebab'. However, this kebab is not cooked in the oven, but in a pan on top of the stove. It is easy to make. It contains a lot of onion but the amount can be reduced.

6 fl oz (175 ml) vegetable oil	2 tsp ground coriander
2 lb (900 g) onions, chopped	salt and pepper
or finely sliced	1 lb (450 g) tomatoes, skinned
2 lb (900 g) lamb on the bone,	and chopped, or
cut into serving-sized pieces	8 fl oz (225 ml) water

Heat the oil in a large pan and add half of the onions. Fry over a medium to high heat until reddish-brown. Add the meat and fry further until the meat is browned, stirring frequently. Add the coriander, salt and pepper. Cook over a medium heat for 15 minutes, then add the rest of the onions and the tomatoes or water. Stir well, cover and cook until the meat is tender. There should not be too much liquid. If there is, uncover the pan and cook further to reduce it.

KEBAB-E-MURGH
Chicken kebab   serves 4

On special occasions, such as an engagement or wedding party, kebabs are prepared with chicken.

1 medium chicken
4 fl oz (110 ml) vegetable oil
2-3 cloves of garlic, peeled
   and crushed

2-3 tbs tomato purée
salt and pepper
fresh mint or coriander for
   garnishing

Rub the prepared chicken with about half of the oil, and with salt and pepper and the garlic.

Cook in a preheated oven at 180°C (350°F, mark 4) or on a rotisserie for about 1½ to 2 hours or until browned, cooked through and tender. During the last half hour of cooking, mix the remaining oil and tomato purée together and spoon over the chicken. Baste frequently.

Serve hot with *nan* or *chappatti* and garnish with fresh mint or coriander.

KEBAB-E-MURGH 2
Chicken kebab   serves 4-6

1 medium chicken
juice of half a lemon, diluted
   with a little water
1 small onion, finely chopped

2 cloves of garlic, peeled and
   crushed
salt and pepper
oil for cooking

Cut the chicken up into serving sized pieces and marinate in the lemon juice, onion, garlic, salt and pepper. Leave in the refrigerator or a cool place for 4-6 hours.

Fry the chicken pieces in hot oil over a medium heat until brown and cooked through. Serve on *nan* or *chappatti*, garnished with fresh mint or coriander.

Alternatively, preheat the grill, brush the chicken pieces with oil and grill under a medium to high heat for 20 minutes, then turn over, brush with oil again and grill for a further 20-30 minutes.

QORMA RUI NAN
Meat stew with leeks and bread   serves 4-6

This tasty dish is a good way to use up left over *nan*. Beef can be used instead of lamb. In Afghanistan *gandana* (Chinese chives, p 40) are used, but leeks are a good substitute.

¼ pint (150 ml) vegetable oil
1 large onion, chopped
1 lb (450 g) boneless lamb, cut into ½" (1 cm) cubes, or 1lb (450 g) minced lamb
¼ pint (150 ml) tomato juice or water

salt
½ tsp black pepper
15 fl oz (425 ml) yoghurt
1 lb (450 g) leeks
2 *nan*
¼-½ tsp red pepper
1 tbs dried mint

Heat half of the vegetable oil in a pan over a medium to high heat. Fry the chopped onion, stirring continuously until reddish-brown. Add the meat, stir well and fry until brown. Add the tomato juice or water and bring to the boil, season with salt and black pepper, stir well, then turn down the heat to low and simmer until the meat is cooked. If necessary add more water. The sauce should be thick and any excess oil can be spooned off.

While the meat is cooking, strain the yoghurt for about an hour to make *chaka* (p 38). Wash and chop up the leeks finely, and drain them well.

When the meat is cooked, and the *chaka* ready, cut the *nan* into 4" (10 cm) triangles or squares and fry in the remaining oil until lightly browned but not too crisp. Keep warm. Fry the leeks in the remaining oil, adding a little extra if necessary; season with a little salt and pepper to taste.

To serve, cover the bottom of a large, warmed dish with about half of the *chaka*, then cover with most of the fried *nan*. Top with the leeks, add the remaining *chaka*, and lastly add the meat. Garnish with the remaining *nan* and sprinkle with the red pepper and the mint. Serve hot.

DO PIAZA
Boiled lamb with onions, on bread   serves 4

Do piaza literally means two onions. The lamb is boiled with red onions and then served garnished with white onions, sliced and marinated in white vinegar. Afghans like this dish to be quite fatty, but the fat can be removed. They also serve it liberally sprinkled with freshly ground black pepper—another matter for individual taste. *Do piaza* is usually served on large *chappatti* or *lawausha* but *nan* can be substituted. It is an ideal dish for buffet parties as the meat can be cooked in advance and it can be served hot or cold.

1 large white onion, finely sliced in rings
¼ pint (150 ml) white vinegar
2 lb (900 g) lamb on the bone, preferably with plenty of fat
2 medium red onions, finely chopped (if necessary substitute white onions)

2 oz (50 g) split yellow peas
1 pint (570 ml) water
salt and pepper
chappatti, lawausha or *nan,* made with 1 lb (450 g) flour

Marinate the white onion rings in the vinegar for at least 2 hours. (If the vinegar is strong, dilute with water.)

Put the lamb, red onions, and split peas in a pan and cover with about 1 pint of water. Season with salt and pepper. Bring to the boil, skimming off the froth from the peas. Turn down the heat and simmer until the meat is tender and the split peas are cooked and soft.

When you are ready to serve, remove the meat and split peas from the soup with a slotted spoon and place on half of the *chappatti* or *nan.* Drain the vinegar from the white onions and place them on top of the lamb and split peas. Sprinkle plenty of freshly ground pepper, then cover with the remaining *chappatti* or *nan.* (The remaining soup can be kept as stock.)

Main Dishes

RICE

All the recipes in this chapter are served with rice. Afghans love it, and their many rice dishes, especially the *pilau* ones, are renowned for their delicious flavours. Two types of rice are used —long grain and short grain. The long grain is used for *pilau* and *chalau* (pp 85-109), the short grain for *bata*, *shola* and rice desserts (pp 110-13, 130-3).

Chalau is a basic dish of white long grain rice. It is cooked very simply with water, a little oil, salt, and sometimes added spices, the most common one being cumin. *Chalau* is usually accompanied by a vegetable or a meat dish.

Pilau, in contrast, is cooked with meat and meat juices, and the rice is always coloured by one method or another. The most common agents for colouring *pilau* are browned onions or caramelised sugar, but saffron and turmeric are also used. A *pilau* normally has some sort of meat buried in the centre of the rice. If using chicken for their *pilau*, Afghans usually cook it whole and serve it whole under the rice. (If you do this, you must choose a pan or casserole large enough to take the whole chicken with the rice, and you may have a problem when it comes to serving out portions to guests.)

Afghans, by the way, cook huge quantities of rice, with relatively little meat, and use more oil in cooking rice than people in the west. In my recipes I have already adjusted quantities to allow for this, but they can of course be further adjusted.

Pots for cooking rice

COOKING LONG GRAIN RICE
Afghans use two methods for cooking long grain rice.

DAMPOKHT METHOD. The rice is boiled in just enough liquid (water or stock) for the cooking. Oil and spices are added to the water at the beginning of the cooking. The rice is finished off in the oven or on top of the stove.

SOF METHOD. The rice is parboiled in a large amount of salted water, then the water is drained off. Oil, more liquid (water or stock) and spices are added at this stage, before the cooking is completed, and the rice is then finished off in the oven or on top of the stove.

Not many Afghans have ovens, especially in the provinces, and the traditional way of cooking rice is in a large *dayg* (cooking pot) over wood or charcoal. Hot coals are placed on top of the lid of the pot to ensure an even heat to dry off the rice.

However, many Afghans nowadays finish off their rice on top of the cooker. They often place a thick, clean cloth over the pan or pot before putting on the lid. The cloth absorbs extra moisture and is also a help if the lid does not fit tightly. They also make several holes in the rice with their *kafgeer* before covering the pan; these holes allow steam to escape.

Which method—*dampokht* or *sof*—is used for cooking *chalau* or *pilau* depends very much on the individual; choose the one you find simplest and which gives the best results for you. The two methods do not produce startlingly different results and are really interchangeable. My Afghan family tended to use the *dampokht* method, but many Afghans prefer the *sof* method as it is less likely to leave the rice sticky.

There is something to be added about the *sof* method. Many Afghans, when they add the meat juices, or water, with the spices and oil, boil the rice again for a couple of minutes over a high heat with the lid on, until the rice catches on the bottom of the pan and a ticking noise is heard. This results in a crust of rice being formed at the bottom of the pan. This crispy rice is called *tie daygi*. After the rice has been served, the *tie daygi* is scraped off the bottom of the pan and served on a separate plate. It is considered a delicacy. However, this method can easily result in burned rice and a ruined pan! You must stay by the pan and listen carefully for the ticking noise.

A little *tie daygi* is usually formed anyway, and this applies to rice cooked by the *dampokht* method too. What I have just explained is how to obtain much more than the usual small amount.

Here are a few general tips for cooking long grain rice.

¶ Always use a heavy pot or pan with a tightly fitting lid, preferably one which can be put in the oven. I have found my cast iron casserole invaluable for cooking rice.

¶ I use basmati rice for all the long grain rice dishes, as it is similar in flavour to that cooked in Afghanistan.

¶ Check the rice for any 'unwanted objects' such as stones, and always wash it several times in cold water until it remains clear. this helps to get rid of surplus starch, besides ensuring clean rice.

¶ Soak the rice for at least half an hour before cooking. Afghans usually prepare and soak their rice for several hours beforehand. The soaking, like the washing, helps to get rid of starch and separates the grains. For *chalau*, some people use the Persian custom of adding a little salt to the water; this helps to whiten the rice.

¶ Before you put the rice into the boiling water, drain it as thoroughly as possible; and do not stir it too vigorously.

¶ When using the *sof* method, remember that the parboiling stage takes only 2-3 minutes; otherwise the rice will be 'mushy' and sticky.

¶ For finishing off the rice, to ensure that the grains are separate and fluffy, and have fully absorbed any added flavours, I recommend using a casserole in the oven. It can be done in a tightly covered pan on top of the stove, but do take care to use the lowest possible heat (and perhaps even raise the pan up on a wok ring).

¶ When Afghans remove rice for serving, they use a *kafgeer*. This large, slotted, flat spoon is used to scrape the rice out very gently, layer by layer. This helps to separate the grains and to keep them from being broken. When the rice is on the serving dish, any lumps are smoothed out by pressing gently with the *kafgeer*.

COOKING SHORT GRAIN RICE
The short grain rice dishes of Afghanistan resemble an Italian risotto; their origins are ancient, from somewhere along the old Silk Route.

The basic short grain rice dish is called *bata*. The rice is cooked with plenty of water until soft and sticky. *Shola*, another and more popular and tasty dish, is cooked with meat and pulses. *Ketcheree quroot* is perhaps the most famous short grain rice dish. It is cooked with *maush* (mung beans) and then served with *qorma* or *kofta*, and with *quroot*, the dried sour yoghurt which is reconstituted with water.

MEAT, FISH AND POULTRY
Lamb, beef, veal, goat, water-buffalo and camel are all cooked in Afghanistan, but lamb is the favourite. Because of the Muslim dietary laws, pork is not eaten. All parts of the animal are cooked, and I should mention here that some Afghan dishes have not been included in this book as they would be too difficult to make in, say, Britain. For example, *landi pilau* is not included. *Landi* is a special type of dried meat. A fat sheep is slaughtered at the end of autumn and the wool is sheared off, leaving the skin with a thick layer of fat underneath. The carcase is then hung to dry. Other dried meat, called *gosht-e-qagh*, is also prepared. Drying is done in the summer months, when livestock is plentiful, and the meat kept for use in the winter.

Another *pilau* left out is *cala pilau*, rice cooked with the head (*cala*) and feet of an animal. There is also *qau*, a whole young lamb roasted in a *tandoor* oven for weddings and special occasions.

Meat is cooked with or without bone. For stews and soups, meat on the bone is preferred as it enhances the flavour and texture of the sauce. Many Afghans like to eat the marrow from a cooked bone.

Poultry, especially chicken, is liked but expensive, so usually reserved for guests and special occasions.

Game such as gazelle, ibex, duck, quail, pigeon and partridge, when available, is prized.

Afghanistan is land-locked, so sea fish are not a regular part of the diet, but in the winter months some are imported from

Pakistan and sold in the bazaars. Shellfish are never eaten.
River fish such as rainbow trout can be found north of the
Hindu Kush, especially in the Salang river, except during the
winter when the rivers are frozen over. South of the Hindu Kush
only brown trout are caught. Carp is also available, from the
Daruntah dam near Jalalabad. The most common fish on sale
in the bazaars in winter is *mahi laqa*, a large catfish found in the
Kunduz river.

PILAU
Yellow rice by the sof *method*   serves 4

This basic *pilau* is quick and simple and can be served with a
meat or vegetable stew.

1 lb (450 g) white long grain rice	1-2 tsp *char marsala* (p 34) or ground cumin
4 tsp sugar	2½ pints (1.5 litre) more water
4 fl oz (110 ml) water	
3 fl oz (75 ml) vegetable oil	salt

Measure out the rice and wash several times in cold clean water
until it runs clear. Add fresh water and soak the rice for at least
half an hour and preferably longer.

Place the sugar in a large pan and stir over a medium to high
heat until it melts and turns a dark golden brown. Remove the
pan from the heat and carefully add the 4 fl oz of water. Then
add the oil, spices and salt. Stir well, and keep warm over a
medium to low heat.

Bring to the boil in a large pan the 2½ pints of water. Add 1
teaspoon of salt. Drain the rice thoroughly and add to the boiling
water. Parboil for 2-3 minutes. Drain in a larve sieve or colander
and put in a casserole with a tightly fitting lid.

Pour the water, sugar and oil over the rice and stir carefully.
Cover with the lid and put in a preheated oven at 150°C (300°F,
mark 2) for about 45 minutes. Alternatively, the rice can be
finished off in a pan over a low heat, for the same length of time.

PILAU
Yellow rice by the dampokht *method*   serves 4

1 lb (450 g) white long grain rice	3 fl oz (75 ml) vegetable oil
4 tsp sugar	1-2 tsp *char marsala* (p 34) or ground cumin
1 pint (570 ml) water or stock	salt

Rinse the rice several times in cold water until it remains clear. Add fresh water and soak the rice for at least half an hour and preferably longer.

Place the sugar in a large flame-proof casserole and stir over a medium to high heat until the sugar dissolves and turns dark golden brown. Remove from the heat while you add the water or stock, the oil, spices and salt, then bring back to the boil. Drain the rice thoroughly, add it to the boiling liquid, and continue boiling over a medium to high heat, with the lid on, until the liquid has evaporated and the rice is 'al dente'. Then stir once, very carefully so as not to break the rice, cover with the lid and put in a preheated oven at 150°C (300°F, mark 2) for 20-30 minutes. Alternatively, the rice can be finished off in a tightly covered pan over a very low heat for the same length of time.

YAKHNI PILAU
Rice with boiled meat serves 4-6

Yakhni means boiled or steamed and this *pilau* is often made for people who are ill or sick because the meat and onions are not fried in oil and are therefore easy to digest. If using lamb, trim off excess fat. This recipe uses the *dampokht* method for cooking the rice.

1 lb (450 g) white long grain rice, preferably basmati
1 1/2-2 lb (700-900 g) lamb on the bone or 1 chicken, cut into pieces
1 pint (570 ml) water

2 medium onions, chopped
2 oz (50 g) carrots, chopped into 1" (2.5 cm) pieces)
2 tsp *char marsala* (p 34)
1/4 tsp saffron (optional)
salt and pepper

Rinse the rice several times in cold water until it remains clear. Add fresh water and leave the rice to soak for at least half an hour.

Put the meat in a casserole and cover with the water. Bring to the boil and skim off any froth which forms. Add the chopped onions and carrots. Sprinkle with the salt and pepper, reduce the heat, and simmer until the meat is tender.

Remove the meat from the casserole and reserve. Strain the stock and measure out 1 pint of it back into the casserole. Drain the rice well and add it, followed by the meat and vegetables; the rice and meat should be covered by about 1/2" (1 cm) of stock. Add the spices, bring to the boil, cover with a lid, turn down the heat slightly, and boil until the rice is tender and the liquid has evaporated. To finish off the rice, place the casserole with the lid tightly on in a preheated oven at 150°C (300°F, mark 2) for 20-30 minutes; or leave it in a tightly covered pan on top of the stove, over a very low heat, for the same length of time.

To serve, mound the rice, meat and carrots on to a large dish.

QABILI PILAU
Yellow rice with carrots and raisins   serves 4-6

This *pilau* is probably the best known and most popular. Any *pilau*, including this one, can be served as a meal on its own or can be served with a *qorma* or vegetable dish. If you use lamb which is fatty, trim off the excess fat, otherwise the *pilau* will be too greasy. This recipe uses the *sof* method of cooking the rice.

1 lb (450 g) long grain rice, preferably basmati
4 fl oz (110 ml) vegetable oil
8 oz (225 g) onions, chopped
1 ½-2 lb (700-900 g) lamb on the bone or 1 chicken, cut in pieces
½ pint (275 ml) water
2 large carrots
4 oz (110 g) black seedless raisins
2 tsp *char marsala* (p 34) or cumin
¼ tsp saffron (optional)
2 ½ pints (1 ½ litres) water
salt and pepper

Rinse the rice several times in cold water until it remains clear. Add fresh water and leave the rice to soak for at least half an hour, preferably longer.

Heat 3 fl oz of the vegetable oil in a large pan and add the chopped onions. Stir and fry them until brown. Remove from the oil and add the lamb or chicken. Brown well on all sides in the oil. Add about ½ pint of water, and salt and pepper. Bring to the boil, then turn down the heat, cover and simmer until the meat is tender. When cooked, remove the meat and put it in a warm place. Grind the onions to a pulp, add them to the meat broth and stir well. Reserve.

While the meat is cooking, wash and peel the carrots and cut into pieces the size of a matchstick. Heat the remaining 1 fl oz of oil in a small pan and add the carrots. Cook the carrots gently until they are lightly browned and tender. If they are tough it may be necessary to add a little water and simmer until tender. All the water should evaporate. Remove the carrots from the oil, add the raisins, and cook these gently until they begin to swell up. Remove from the oil and set aside with the carrots. Save any remaining oil for the rice.

Bring to the boil 2 ½ pints of water and add about 1 teaspoon of salt. Drain the rice and add to the boiling water. Parboil for

2-3 minutes before draining the rice in a large sieve. Put the rice in a large casserole and sprinkle with the spices and saffron (if used). Take the meat juices and measure out approximately 8 fl oz. Pour the juices over the rice and stir very gently once. Then place the cooked meat on one side of the casserole and the carrots and raisins on the other. Add any oil left over from cooking the carrots. Cover with a tightly fitting lid and place in a preheated oven at 150°C (300°F, mark 2) for about 45 minutes or leave it in a tightly covered pan on top of the stove over a very low heat for the same length of time.

To serve, remove the carrots and raisins and set to one side. Remove the meat and set to one side. Take about a quarter of the rice and put on a large dish. Top with the meat, then cover with the remaining rice. Garnish the top of the rice with the carrots and raisins.

QABILI PILAU UZBEKI
Uzbek rice with carrots and raisins   serves 4-6

This is *Qabili pilau* prepared by the Uzbeks using the *dampokht* method of cooking rice. It is, I think, a quicker and simpler way than the *sof* method. The recipe was given to me by Mrs Rashidzada, an Uzbek lady.

1 lb (450 g) long grain rice, preferably basmati	water
	2 large carrots
4 fl oz (110 ml) vegetable oil	4 oz (110 g) raisins
2 medium onions, chopped	2 tsp ground cumin
1½-2 lb (700-900 g) lamb on the bone or 1 chicken, cut in pieces	1 tsp black pepper
	salt

Rinse the rice several times until the water remains clear, then leave it to soak in fresh water for at least half an hour.

Heat the oil in a flame-proof casserole over a medium to high heat and add the chopped onions. Fry until golden brown and soft. Add the meat (if lamb, trimmed of excess fat) and fry until well browned. Then add enough water to cover the meat, and salt, bring to the boil, turn down the heat, and cook gently until the meat is tender.

While the meat is cooking, wash, peel and cut up the carrots into pieces like matchsticks.

When the meat is done and you are ready to cook the rice, add the carrots and the raisins to the top of the meat, sprinkle with 1 teaspoon each of cumin and black pepper, and salt.

Drain the rice, place it on top of the carrots and raisins, and add enough water to cover it by about ½" (1 cm). Add the other teaspoon of cumin and a little salt, bring to the boil, turn down the heat, cover, and boil gently for about 10 minutes until the rice is tender and the water absorbed. It is important that you listen carefully while cooking this rice for a ticking noise. When you hear it, remove the pan immediately from the heat (as explained on p 82).

Place the casserole, which should have a tightly fitting lid, in a preheated oven at 150°C (300°F, mark 2) for about 45 minutes. Or you can finish the cooking by leaving it over a very low heat on top of the stove for the same length of time.

To serve, mound the rice, meat, carrots and raisins on to a large dish.

KOFTA PILAU
Yellow rice and meatballs   serves 4-6

This recipe is one of those which use the *sof* method for cooking the rice.

1 lb (450 g) long grain white rice, *preferably basmati*	*for meatballs and sauce* see ingredients lists
2½ pints (1.5 litre) water, and a little more	given on p 105
2 tsp *char marsala* (p 34)	

Rinse the rice several times in cold water until it remains clear. Add fresh water and leave the rice to soak for at least half an hour.

Cook the meatballs and sauce as in the recipe for *Kofta chalau* (p 105), but omitting the yoghurt.

Bring to the boil the 2½ pints of water with about 1 teaspoon of salt. Drain the rice and add to the boiling water. Parboil for 2-3 minutes. Drain the rice in a large sieve.

Put half of the rice in a large casserole with a tightly fitting lid and then add the meatballs with the rest of the rice on top. Make up the sauce of the meatballs to 8 fl oz with a little more water, add it to the rice, and sprinkle the *char marsala* on top of the rice. Mix gently, taking care not to break the meatballs. Cover and put into a preheated oven at 150°C (300°F, mark 2) for about 45 minutes; or leave over a very low heat on top of the stove for the same length of time.

When serving, the meatballs are mixed in with the rice.

YAHKOOT PILAU or BONJON-E-RHUMI PILAU
Rice with tomatoes serves 4-6

The tomatoes in this recipe colour the rice to a reddish colour; hence its name, *yahkoot* meaning ruby. If using lamb, trim off excess fat before cooking. The *dampokht* method is followed for cooking the rice.

1 lb (450 g) long grain white rice, preferably basmati
2 medium onions, chopped
4 fl oz (110 ml) vegetable oil
1 ½-2 lb (700-900 g) lamb or chicken on the bone, cut into pieces
2 cloves of garlic, peeled and crushed
1 tsp turmeric
1 lb (450 g) tomatoes, skinned and chopped
½ oz (15 g) sugar
salt
pepper
½ tsp ground green or white cardamom seeds

Measure out the rice and rinse several times until the water remains clear. Add fresh water and leave the rice to soak for at least half an hour.

Fry the chopped onions in the oil until reddish-brown, then add the meat, crushed garlic and turmeric. Fry until the meat is well browned. Add the tomatoes, sugar, salt and pepper. Do not add any water. Stir well and boil for about 5 minutes, then turn down the heat and simmer until the meat is tender.

Drain the rice and put half of it in large casserole with a tightly fitting lid. Add the meat and tomatoes and then top with the rest of the rice and the ground cardamom, stir well. Add extra water, if needed, to bring the level of liquid to about ½" (1 cm) above the rice. Bring to the boil, then turn down the heat a little and simmer for about 10 minutes until the rice is tender and the all the liquid has evaporated. If the liquid has evaporated and the rice is not cooked, add a little more water and cook until the additional water has been absorbed. Cover with the lid and put in a preheated oven—150°C (300°F, mark 2)—for 20-30 minutes. The rice can be cooked in a tightly covered pan over a very low heat for the same length of time, if you prefer.

To serve, mound the rice and meat on a large warm dish.

QORMA PILAU
Yellow rice and meat stew   serves 4-6

This recipe uses the *sof* method of cooking rice. If using lamb, trim off excess fat before cooking.

1 lb (450 g) long grain white rice, preferably basmati	½ tsp ground black cardamom
4 fl oz (110 ml) vegetable oil	1 hot green pepper (or use ground black pepper)
2 medium onions, chopped	1 tsp green or white cardamom seeds, ground
1½-2 lb (700-900 g) lamb on the bone or 1 chicken, cut into pieces	½ tsp saffron
1½ oz (40 g) yellow split peas	1 tsp ground cumin
8 fl oz (225 ml) water	salt
	2½ pints (1.5 litre) water

Rinse the rice several times until the water remains clear, and leave it to soak in fresh water for at least half an hour.

Heat the oil in a large pan and fry the chopped onions over a medium to high heat until reddish-brown. Remove the onions and set to one side. Add the meat to the oil and fry until well browned all over. Add the fried onions, split peas and the 8 fl oz of water (or sufficient to cover the meat). Add the ground black cardamom seeds, and salt. Cook slowly over a low to medium heat until the meat and peas are tender. Add the hot pepper or black pepper, the ground cardamom seeds and half of the saffron.

Bring to the boil in a large casserole with a tightly fitting lid the 2½ pints of salted water. Drain the rice, add it to the boiling water, parboil it for 2-3 minutes, then drain it again in a large sieve.

Place about half of the rice back in the casserole, add the meat, peas, the remaining saffron, diluted in a little water, and the ground cumin. Add the rest of the rice on top. Measure out about 8 fl oz (225 ml) of meat juices and pour over the rice. Top with a tightly fitting lid and place in a preheated oven at 150°C (300°F, mark 2) for about 45 minutes; or leave it over a very low heat on top of the stove for the same length of time.

BONJON PILAU
Yellow rice with aubergines serves 4-6

This is a rich and spicy *pilau*. The *sof* method is used for cooking the rice.

1 lb (450 g) long grain white rice, preferably basmati	8 fl oz (225 ml) water, plus 2½ pints (1½ litres)
1 lb (450 g) aubergines	2 cloves of garlic, peeled and crushed
6 fl oz (175 ml) vegetable oil	
2 medium onions, chopped	1 tsp turmeric
1½-2 lb (700-900 g) lamb or beef on the bone, cut into pieces	1 tsp ground coriander
	½ tsp saffron
	salt and black or red pepper

Rinse the rice several times until the water remains clear, then leave it to soak in fresh water for at least half an hour.

Peel and slice the aubergines lengthwise to about ½″ (1 cm) thickness. Spread them on a plate, sprinkle with salt (see p 40) and set aside for about half an hour.

Heat 2 fl oz (4 tablespoons) of the oil in a pan and fry the chopped onions over a medium heat until golden brown and soft, then put in the meat (if lamb, trimmed of excess fat) and fry until well browned, stirring frequently. Add the 8 fl oz water, salt and pepper, and bring to the boil. Stir, then lower the heat and cook until the meat is tender.

Meanwhile rinse the aubergines and pat dry with a clean cloth or kitchen paper. Heat the remaining oil in a large frying-pan and fry the aubergines on both sides until golden. You may need more oil as they tend to soak it up during cooking, but drain them thoroughly otherwise the rice will be too oily. Reserve the aubergines.

Mix the garlic, turmeric and coriander together in a little water and add to the aubergines. Add to this 8 fl oz (225 ml) of juices from the meat and simmer over a low heat for about half an hour.

Bring to the boil the 2½ pints of water, with salt. Drain the rice, put it into the boiling water, parboil it (2-3 minutes), then drain it in a large sieve. Next, put half the rice in a large casserole which has a tightly fitting lid, and add the meat.

Sprinkle with red or black pepper, according to taste, cover with a little more of the rice, add the aubergines, then top with the remaining rice. Add the saffron to the remaining juices from the meat and aubergines and pour over the rice. Cover with the lid and put in a preheated oven at 150°C (300°F, mark 2) for about 45 minutes; or leave it over a very low heat on top of the stove for the same length of time.

To serve, remove the top layer of rice and place on a warm dish. Cover with the meat and aubergines and then add the remaining rice.

ZAMARUD or SABZI PILAU
Rice with spinach   serves 4-6

A beautiful green dish; *zamarud* means emerald.

1 lb (450 g) long grain white rice, preferably basmati	2 tsp *char marsala* (p 34)
5 fl oz (150 ml) vegetable oil	1 lb (450 g) spinach
2 medium onions, chopped	4 oz (110 g) leeks or
1½-2 lb (700-900 g) lamb on the bone, or 1 chicken, cut into pieces	*gandana* (p 40)
	2 tsp powdered dill weed
	salt and pepper
	2½ pints (1.5 litre) water
8 fl oz (225 ml) water	1 hot green pepper

Rinse the rice several times until the water remains clear, then leave it to soak in fresh water for at least half an hour.

Now, the meat. If using lamb trim off excess fat. Heat 4 fl oz (110 ml) of the oil in a pan and fry the onions in it, stirring frequently until golden brown and soft. Add the lamb or chicken and continue frying until the meat and onions are well browned. Next, add the 8 fl oz of water, 1 teaspoon of the *char marsala*, salt and plenty of black pepper, bring to the boil, turn down the heat, stir well, and simmer until the meat is tender.

Now prepare the spinach as for *sabzi chalau* (p 109). Wash and thoroughly drain the spinach. Cut the leeks into small pieces and wash thoroughly. Chop up the spinach. Heat the remaining oil in a large pan and fry the leeks in it, until they are soft and nearly brown, then add the spinach and continue to fry, stirring continuously, until it reduces in size. Reduce the heat, cover the pan, and simmer until the spinach is cooked. Then add the dill, salt and pepper, cover again and continue to cook gently until all water has evaporated and the spinach is creamy and soft.

Bring to the boil the 2½ pints of water with about 1 teaspoon of salt, drain the rice and put it in the boiling water. Parboil it for 2-3 minutes, then drain it in a large sieve and transfer it to a large casserole with a tightly fitting lid. Add the cooked spinach, the meat with 8 fl oz (225 ml) of the juices and 1 teaspoon of *char marsala*. Mix gently but thoroughly. Place the hot pepper on top of the rice, cover and put in a preheated oven—150°C (300°F, mark 2)—for about 45 minutes.

MAUSH PILAU
Rice, mung beans and apricots serves 6-8

This *pilau* is often cooked without meat. The apricots make an unusual but delicious addition. If using lamb, trim off excess fat before cooking. The *sof* method of cooking rice is used here.

1 lb (450 g) long grain white rice, preferably basmati	2 lb (900 g) lamb or beef on the bone, cut into pieces
5 oz (150 g) mung beans	8 fl oz (225 ml) water, plus
5 oz (150 g) dried apricots (optional), soaked overnight	3 pints (1.75 litres)
	2 tsp ground cumin or
4 fl oz (110 ml) vegetable oil	*char marsala* (p 34)
8 oz (225 g) onions, chopped	salt and pepper

Rinse the rice several times until the water remains clear, and leave it to soak in fresh water for at least half an hour. Wash the mung beans and leave them to soak for 1-2 hours.

If using apricots cook them in a little water until they are soft.

Heat the oil in a pan and fry the onions until brown. Remove the onions and add the meat (if lamb, trimmed of excess fat). Brown well in the oil. Add the 8 fl oz water, and salt and pepper, bring to the boil, then turn down the heat, cover, and cook gently until the meat is tender. When cooked, remove the meat and set aside in a warm place. Grind the browned onions to a pulp and add to the meat juices, stirring well.

Bring the 3 pints of water to boil in a large casserole and add the mung beans. Cook them until half done (about 10-15 minutes). Then drain the rice and add it to the mung beans. Bring back to the boil, add salt and cook for 2-3 minutes. Drain the rice and mung beans in a large sieve, then return to the casserole. Sprinkle with the cumin or *char marsala* and add 8 fl oz (225 ml) of the meat juices. Place the meat on top of one side of the rice and, if the apricots are used, place them on the other side. Cover tightly and put in a preheated oven at 150°C (300°F, mark 2) for about 45 minutes; or leave over a very low heat on top of the stove for the same length of time.

Serve the meat on a large dish, topped with the rice and mung beans and garnished with the apricots (if used).

NORINJ PILAU
Rice with orange serves 4-6

Traditionally this *pilau* is prepared with the peel of the bitter (or Seville) oranges. It is quite a sweet dish. My family in Afghanistan made this slightly different recipe which is not so sweet and I much prefer it. I have also used the peel of ordinary oranges which are easier to obtain. *Norinj pilau* is one of my favourite Afghan dishes and it has a lovely delicate flavour. This recipe uses the *dampokht* method of cooking rice. If using lamb, trim off excess fat.

1 lb (450 g) long grain white rice, preferably basmati
4 fl oz (110 ml) vegetable oil
2 medium onions, chopped
1 chicken or 1 1/2-2 lb (700-900 g) lamb on the bone, cut in pieces
1 pint (570 ml) water, plus 4 fl oz (110 ml) water
peel of 1 large orange

2 oz (50 g) sugar
2 oz (50 g) blanched and flaked almonds
2 oz (50 g) blanched and flaked pistachios
1/2 tsp saffron
1 tsp ground green or white cardamom seeds
1 fl oz (25 ml) rose-water
salt and pepper

Measure out the rice and rinse several times until the water remains clear. Add fresh water and leave the rice to soak for at least half an hour.

Heat the oil and add the chopped onions. Stir and fry them over a medium to high heat until golden brown and soft. Add the meat and fry until brown, turning frequently. Add 1 pint of water, salt and pepper and cook gently until the meat is tender.

While the meat is cooking, wash and cut up the peel of 1 large orange into matchstick-sized pieces, removing as much pith as possible. To remove any bitter taste, put the orange strips into a strainer and dip first in boiling water and then cold. Repeat this several times. Set aside.

Make a syrup by bringing to the boil 4 fl oz of water and the 2 oz of sugar. Add the orange peel, the flaked almonds and pistachios to the boiling syrup. Boil for about 5 minutes, skimming off the thick froth when necessary. Strain and set aside the peel and nuts. Add the saffron and rose-water to the syrup and boil again gently for another 3 minutes. Add the ground cardamom.

To cook the rice, strain the chicken stock (setting the meat to one side), and add the syrup. Make the syrup and stock up to 1 pint (570 ml), by adding extra water if necessary. The oil will be on the surface of the stock and this should also be included in the cooking of the rice. Bring the liquid to the boil in a large casserole. Drain the rice and then add it to the boiling liquid. Add salt, the nuts and the peel, reserving about a third for garnishing. Bring back to the boil, then cover with a tightly fitting lid, turn down the heat to medium and boil for about 10 minutes until the rice is tender and all the liquid is absorbed.

Add the meat, the remaining peel and nuts on top of the rice and cover with the tightly fitting lid. Put into a preheated oven—150°C (300°F, mark 2)—for 20-30 minutes. Or cook over a very low heat for the same length of time.

When serving, place the meat in the centre of a large dish, mound the rice over the top and then garnish with the orange peel and nuts.

ZARDA PILAU
Yellow rice, nuts and saffron   serves 4-6

The saffron gives the rice a yellow colour, hence its name, *zard* meaning yellow. It is usually only prepared for special guests or for special occasions. If using lamb, trim off excess fat. This recipe uses the *sof* method of cooking rice.

1 lb (450 g) long grain white
  rice, preferably basmati
4 fl oz (110 ml) vegetable oil
8oz (225 g) onions, chopped
1 ½-2 lb (700-900 g) lamb on
  the bone, or 1 chicken, cut
  in pieces
½ pint (275 ml) water, plus
  4 fl oz (110 ml) water
2 oz (50 g) sugar

1 oz (25 g) pistachios,
  skinned and flaked
1 oz (25 g) almonds,
  skinned and flaked
½ tsp saffron
2 ½ pints (1 ½ litres) water
2 tsp *char marsala* (p 34)
salt
pepper

Rinse the rice several times until the water remains clear. Add fresh water and leave the rice to soak for at least half an hour, preferably longer.

Heat the vegetable oil in a large casserole and add the chopped onions. Stir and fry until they are golden brown. Add the lamb or chicken and brown well on all sides. Add about ½ pint of water and salt and pepper, Cover and bring to the boil, then turn down the heat and simmer until the meat is tender. Remove the meat and set aside, preferably in a warm place.

Shortly before you are ready to cook the rice, make a syrup with the 4 fl oz of water and the 2 oz of sugar. Put them in a pan and bring to the boil. Boil until syrupy (about 5 minutes). Add the pistachios, almonds and saffron. Keep warm.

Bring to the boil 2 ½ pints (1 ½ litres) of water and 1 teaspoon of salt. Drain the rice and put into the boiling water. Parboil the rice for 2-3 minutes. Drain it in a large sieve. Mix gently approximately one quarter of the rice into the warm syrup. Put the remaining rice in a large casserole, sprinkle with the *char marsala*.

Take the meat juices and measure out approximately 8 fl oz

(225 ml) and pour them over the rice. Top the rice on one side with the meat and put the rice containing the nuts on the other side. Cover with a tightly fitting lid. Put the casserole into a preheated oven—150°C (300°F, mark 2)—for about 45 minutes. Cook in a pan over a very low heat for the same length of time, if you prefer.

To serve, remove the meat and set to one side. Next remove the rice containing the nuts and set aside. Then take about one quarter of the remaining rice and put on a large dish. Top with the meat, then cover with the remaining rice. Garnish the top with the nuts mixed with rice.

RESHTA PILAU
Rice with vermicelli   serves 4

Reshta is the Arabic name for noodles and in Dari it means thread. In Afghanistan, *reshta pilau* is a sweet *pilau* made with fine egg vermicelli. This recipe does not contain meat but it can be eaten with a stew (*qorma*) or vegetable dish.

1 lb (450 g) long grain white rice, preferably basmati	8 fl oz (225 ml) water, plus 4 fl oz (110 ml)
2½ pints (1.5 litre) of water	7 oz (200 g) sugar
salt	½ tsp saffron
5 fl oz (150 ml) vegetable oil	1 oz (25 g) pistachios, skinned and cut into quarters
8 oz (225 g) fine egg vermicelli broken into lengths of 1-2" (2.5-5 cm)	1 oz (25 g) almonds, skinned and cut into quarters

Wash the rice several times in water until the colour remains clear. Soak the rice in fresh water for at least half an hour, preferably longer.

Bring 2½ pints of water to the boil in a large casserole and add about 1 teaspoon of salt. Drain the rice thoroughly and add to the boiling water. Parboil the rice for about 2-3 minutes. Drain it in a large sieve. Take three quarters of the rice and put into a large casserole covered with a tightly fitting lid. Keep in a warm place. Reserve the remaining quarter of the rice.

Heat half of the vegetable oil in a pan over a medium heat and add the egg vermicelli. Fry gently for a few minutes. Do not brown.

Put the 8 fl oz of water in another pan and add the 7 oz sugar. Bring to the boil and stir over a high heat until a thin syrup forms (about 5 minutes). Add the fried vermicelli, saffron and nuts to this syrup.

Now deal with the reserved quarter of the rice. Take a large spoonful of rice and put in a sieve. Add a large spoonful of the vermicelli mixed with syrup. Repeat, layering in this way until all the rice and vermicelli are in the sieve.

Now assemble the various preparations before the final cooking. Mix together the 4 fl oz of water, the remaining oil and salt. Add this to the three quarters of rice in the casserole, stir once gently and then place the rice and vermicelli mixture from the sieve on top of one side of the plain rice. Do not stir. Cover with the tightly fitting lid and place in a preheated oven—150°C (300°F, mark 2)—for about 45 minutes.

To serve, first remove and reserve the rice and vermicelli mixture and then place the rice on a large dish. Garnish the rice with the vermicelli, sweetened rice and nuts.

CHALAU SOF
White long grain rice   serves 4

Chalau is white long grain rice. It is usually served with a meat or vegetable stew, *qorma*, or meatballs, *kofta*. The basic method for cooking *chalau* the *sof* way is as follows.

1 lb (450 g) white long grain rice
2½ pints (1.5 litre) water, plus 4 fl oz (110 ml) water
salt

2 fl oz (55 ml) vegetable oil
1-2 tsp ground or whole cumin, or *char marsala* (p 34)

Wash the rice several times until the water remains clear. Soak the rice in water for at least half an hour, preferably longer.

Bring the 2½ pints of water to the boil in a large pan. Add salt. Drain the rice and add it to the boiling water. Parboil the rice for about 2-3 minutes. (If you overcook the rice at this stage, the grains will stick together.) Drain the rice in a large sieve or colander and then place the rice in a pan or casserole which has a tightly fitting lid. Mix the oil, 4 fl oz water, spices and salt together gently. Cover with the lid and either place in a preheated oven—150°C (300°F, mark 2)—or over a low heat for 30-45 minutes.

CHALAU DAMPOKHT   serves 4

To cook *chalau* by the *dampokht* method you need exactly the same ingredients as for the *sof* method (see preceding recipe) except that 1 pint of water (570 ml) will be enough.

Bring the 1 pint of water to the boil in a large pan. Drain the rice as much as possible and add to the boiling water. Add the salt, vegetable oil and spices. Bring back to the boil, stir gently once, then cover with the lid and turn the heat down to medium. Boil gently until the rice is 'al dente' and all the water has evaporated. (There will be a ticking noise as the rice 'catches' at the bottom of the pan.) Then put the pan either in a preheated oven at 150°C (300°F, mark 2) or over a very low heat on top of the stove for 20-30 minutes.

QORMA CHALAU
Meat stew with rice   serves 4-6

There are many variations to this dish. Instead of split peas, other pulses such as red kidney beans may be used (soaked overnight and well cooked before being added to the meat). Or substitute fresh vegetables, e.g. potatoes, carrots, cauliflower, peas, green beans, all sliced or diced, added to the *qorma* when the meat is already tender and the sauce thick, and then cooked for about 15 minutes, adding a little extra water if necessary.

4 fl oz (110 ml) vegetable oil	2 oz (50 g) split peas
1 lb (450 g) onions, chopped	1 tsp *char marsala* (p 34)
2 lb (900 g) lamb on the bone,	or ground coriander
beef or chicken, cut in pieces	½ tsp black pepper
1-2 tbs tomato purée	salt
¼-½ pint (150-275 ml) water	red pepper (optional)

Heat the oil in a pan and add the chopped onions. Fry over a medium to high heat, stirring frequently until golden brown and soft. Add the lamb, beef or chicken and fry again until the meat and onions are well browned. Mix in the tomato purée and continue frying for a minute or two. Add the water, split peas, spices, salt and pepper and bring to the boil, then turn the heat down and simmer until the meat is cooked and the split peas soft. The sauce should be thick and oily, but excess oil can be spooned off if wished. Serve with *chalau* (pp 103-4) and garnish the rice with a little of the sauce.

KOFTA CHALAU
Meatballs with rice   serves 4

Kofta chalau is a favourite rice dish. The recipe for the meatballs can also be used with *ketcheree quroot, maushawa* and *aush*.

for the meatballs

1 lb (450 g) minced beef or lamb	1 egg (optional)
	1-2 tsp ground coriander
1 medium onion, minced or ground	1 tsp *char marsala* (p 34, optional)
2 cloves of garlic, peeled and crushed	½ tsp black pepper
	salt

for the sauce

3 fl oz (75 ml) vegetable oil	water
2 medium onions, finely chopped	salt
	red or black pepper
4 oz (110 g) tomatoes, skinned and chopped	4 fl oz (110 ml) strained yoghurt

Combine and mix together all the ingredients for the meatballs thoroughly and shape into balls about 1-2" (2.5-5 cm) in diameter. Flatten the balls slightly.

Heat the oil in a pan over a medium to high heat. Add the chopped onions and fry, stirring continuously until they are reddish-brown. Add the chopped tomatoes and stir and fry briskly until the sauce turns brownish. Add salt and pepper. Stir in a little water. Bring to the boiling point and then add the meatballs, one at a time, in a single layer. Add more water if necessary to just cover the meatballs. Afterwards cover, but leave the lid slightly ajar. Turn the heat down to low and simmer gently for about an hour or until the meatballs and sauce are brown and the sauce thick. Add the strained yoghurt and stir it into the sauce carefully. Serve with *chalau*.

MAHI CHALAU
Fish stew with rice   serves 4-6

The large river fish, *mahi laqa*, found in the Kunduz river and used for this dish is similar in taste and texture to cod or haddock, either of which can be substituted in this recipe.

Jelabi, originating from India, are often eaten as a sweet after eating fish in the winter months. In winter, fish are displayed in the bazaars alongside mountains of *jelabi*.

2 lb (900 g) fish (see above)
3 fl oz (75 ml) vegetable oil
7 oz (200 g) onions, chopped
3 cloves of garlic, peeled and
   crushed
1 large can of tomatoes (400 g,
   14 oz), chopped

10 fl oz (275 ml) water
½ tsp ground coriander
1 tsp turmeric
red pepper
salt

Cut the fish into large chunks. Pat dry with kitchen paper. Heat the oil in a pan and fry the fish quickly over a high heat on both sides until golden brown. Do not cook through. Remove the fish from the pan and set to one side.

Filter the oil and put into a deep pan. Heat the oil again and fry the chopped onions and crushed garlic over a medium to high heat until soft and reddish-brown. Mix in the tomatoes and fry vigorously until the tomatoes brown and the liquid reduces. Add the water, coriander, turmeric, red pepper and salt. Stir, cover, turn down the heat and simmer for about half an hour. Add the fish and simmer for a further 15-30 minutes. Do not overcook or boil vigorously, or the fish will disintegrate.

Serve with *chalau* (or with *bata*, p 110).

ZAMARUD CHALAU
Emerald (spinach) rice   serves 4

This recipe differs from *Sabzi chalau* in that the rice is actually cooked in the spinach water. This gives the rice a green colour and its name, *zamarud*, meaning emerald. This was one of my favourites when I lived in Afghanistan. It can be served with *kofta* or *qorma*. The spinach should be very fresh so that the rice becomes a good green colour.

1 lb (450 g) long grain white rice	1 tbs dried dill weed
2 lb (900 g) spinach	½-1 tbs fenugreek (optional)
¼ pint (150 ml) water, plus 2½ pints (1½ litres)	6 fl oz (175 ml) vegetable oil
8 oz (225 g) leeks (or *gandana* (p 40)	2 tsp cumin, whole or ground
	salt
	black pepper

Rinse the rice several times in cold water until it remains clear. Add fresh water and leave the rice to soak for at least half an hour.

Chop the spinach into small pieces and then wash thoroughly. Drain well. Put the spinach into a large pan and add ¼ pint water. Add 3 fl oz (75 ml) of the oil. Put on a medium to high heat and boil for about 5 minutes, stirring occasionally until the spinach reduces and the water becomes green. Drain off the water and oil from the spinach into a bowl or measuring jug, reserving 4 fl oz (110 ml) of liquid and 3 fl oz (85 ml) of oil for cooking the rice and any remaining liquid for cooking the spinach.

Chop up the leeks into small pieces and wash thoroughly. Heat the remaining 3 fl oz (75 ml) of oil in a pan and add the leeks, which should be well drained. Fry over a medium heat until soft but not brown. Add the leeks to the spinach, then add the dill, fenugreek (if used) and salt and pepper. Cook on a low heat, adding any remaining spinach water (except the 4 fl oz reserved for cooking the rice), until all the water has evaporated and the spinach is soft.

Bring to the boil 2½ pints of water. Drain the rice and add to the boiling water. Parboil for 2-3 minutes, then drain the rice in a colander or large sieve. Put the rice in a casserole which has a tightly fitting lid. Now add the cumin, salt and pepper to the reserved 4 fl oz of spinach water and 3 fl oz of oil and pour over the rice. Stir once gently, then cover with the lid and put in a preheated oven at 150°C (300°F, mark 2) for 30-45 minutes. Alternatively cook over a low heat for the same time.

Serve the rice with the spinach and with a meat dish, if required.

Main Dishes

BONJON CHALAU
Aubergines with rice   serves 4

This is similar to ratatouille. Although commonly served with
chalau, it can also be served with *bata* (p 110).

1 lb (450 g) aubergines	4 fl oz (110 ml) water
5 fl oz (150 ml) vegetable oil	1 tsp ground coriander
1 medium onion, chopped	salt
5 fl oz (150 ml) tomato juice	red or black pepper

Peel and chop the aubergines into 1" (2.5 cm) cubes. Sprinkle
with salt on a board or plate (see p 40) and leave for about half
an hour. Rinse with cold water and wipe dry.

Heat the vegetable oil in a pan and add the chopped onions.
Fry over a medium to high heat until brown. Remove from the
oil and set to one side.

Fry the aubergines in the remaining oil until well browned on
all sides. (You may need a little more oil as aubergines soak up
a lot.) Grind the fried onions to a pulp and add them to the
aubergines. Mix in the tomato juice, water, coriander, salt and
pepper, and then cook gently for about an hour, either on top of
the stove in a pan with a tightly fitting lid or in a casserole in a
preheated oven at 150°C (300°F, mark 2).

Serve with *chalau*. Some people add yoghurt to this dish or
serve a bowl of yoghurt separately.

QORMA-E-OLU BOKHARA
Stew with meat and plums   serves 4

This is the same recipe as the basic *qorma* (*qorma chalau*, p 104),
except that small yellow, tart plums, *olu bokhara*, are added.
These are not available in the west, but canned golden plums
can be substituted. The plums should be drained, stoned and
cut into four before adding to the stew and not more than 3
plums added for 1 lb of meat. If using plums, do not include
fresh vegetables in the stew.

108

SABZI CHALAU
Spinach with rice   serves 4

A combination of spinach with rice, which is often accompanied by meat in the form of a separately cooked *qorma*. *Qorma chalau* (p 104) without the tomato paste would be suitable. The *qorma* would be added to the spinach just before serving, while the rice would be served on a separate platter.

If the dish is made with short grain rice, it becomes *Sabzi bata*, as explained on the next page.

2 lb (900 g) spinach	1 tbs powdered dill weed
8 oz (225 g) leeks or	½-1 tbs fenugreek (optional)
gandana (p 40)	salt
3 fl oz (75 ml) vegetable oil	black pepper

Chop the spinach into small pieces and wash thoroughly. Drain well. Cut up the leeks into small pieces and wash carefully.

Heat the oil and fry the leeks in it until soft and nearly brown. Add the spinach and continue to fry, stirring continuously until it reduces. Then turn the heat down, cover the pan with a lid, and simmer until the spinach is cooked and the oil comes to the surface. At this stage, add dill, the fenugreek (if used), salt and black pepper. Cover again and cook until any excess water has evaporated and the spinach becomes creamy and soft.

Serve with *chalau*.

SHALGHAM CHALAU
Turnip stew with long grain rice   serves 4

Cook the turnip stew as in *Shalgham bata* (p 111), but serve it with *chalau* instead of *bata*.

BATA
Sticky short grain rice   serves 4

This is the basic short grain rice dish. It is served with a variety of stews or vegetables the most common being turnip stew, *Shalgam bata* (see recipe on the next page).

1 lb (450 g) short grain rice   4 fl oz (110 ml) vegetable oil
2½ pints (1.5 litre) water   salt

Wash the rice and put in a pan with the 2½ pints of water. Add salt. Bring to the boil, then turn down the heat and cook gently, adding more water if necessary, until the rice is soft and the water evaporated. Cover with a tightly fitting lid and put in an oven preheated to 150°C (300°F, mark 2) or cook over a low heat for half an hour. Then stir the rice; it should be thick and sticky. Add the oil, cover with the lid, and cook for a further half hour.

BONJON BATA   serves 4

Prepare and cook aubergines as in the recipe for *Bonjon chalau* (p 108). Prepare and cook short grain rice as in the recipe above for *Bata*.

SABZI BATA   serves 4

Prepare and cook spinach as in the recipe for *Sabzi chalau*, on the preceding page. Prepare and cook short grain rice as in the recipe above for *Bata*. The dish can be eaten with a stew (*qorma*) if wished.

SHALGHAM BATA
Turnip stew with rice and lamb   serves 4

This tasty turnip stew is traditionally served with *bata* (see preceding page). It can also be served with *chalau* (pp 103-4).

6 fl oz (175 ml) vegetable oil
6 oz (175 g) onions, chopped
1 ½ lb (700 g) lamb on the
   bone
1 lb (450 g) turnip, chopped
   into 1″ (2.5 cm) cubes
2 tsp ground coriander
2 tsp ground ginger

3 oz (75 g) brown sugar or
   molasses
4 fl oz (110 ml) water, plus
   2 ½ pints (1.5 litre)
¼ tsp saffron
salt and black pepper
1 lb (450 g) white short grain
   rice

Heat the oil in a pan and add the chopped onions. Fry over a medium to high heat until soft and golden brown. Add the meat and fry until the meat is golden brown and then add the chopped turnip and fry until brown. Add the ground coriander, ginger, sugar and salt and pepper. Stir well and add the 4 fl oz of water. Bring to the boil, then turn down the heat and simmer until the meat is cooked and tender, adding more water to prevent sticking, if necessary. The sauce should be quite thick and not runny. The oil comes to the surface when the sauce is cooked.

Meanwhile wash the rice and put in a large pan with the 2 ½ pints of water. Add salt and bring to the boil, then turn down the heat and cook gently until the rice is soft and the water has evaporated. Add more water if necessary. Cover with a tightly fitting lid and put in a preheated oven at 150°C (300°F, mark 2) or cook over a low heat for half an hour. After half an hour, take the lid off and stir the rice. It should be thick and sticky. Spoon off 4 fl oz (110 ml) of oil from the surface of the stew. Add this oil to the rice and stir and mix again. Cover with the lid and cook for a further half hour.

Before serving, add the saffron to the meat and turnips, stir well and leave on a low heat to blend for a minute or two.

Mound the rice on to a large dish, make a well in the centre and fill with some of the juices from the meat and turnips. Put the rest in a separate dish.

SHOLA GOSHTI
Sticky rice with meat   serves 3-4

A recipe with many variations. This version was given to me by Mr A. G. Redja. *Shola* is often made for *Nazer* (p 22).

4 oz (110 g) mung beans (or green lentils)
3 fl oz (75 ml) vegetable oil
1 medium to large onion, finely chopped
8 oz (225 g) boneless lamb or beef, in 3⁄4" (2 cm) cubes
1 tbs tomato purée

3 cloves of garlic, peeled and crushed
1 pint (570 ml) water, plus 1⁄4 pint (150 ml) water
2 tsp powdered dill weed
salt and black pepper
8 oz (225 g) short grain rice
1⁄2 sweet pepper, chopped (optional)
1 tsp *char marsala* (p 34)

Wash the mung beans and soak for half an hour in warm water.

Heat most of the oil (reserve about 1 tablespoon) in a pan and fry the chopped onions in it until reddish-brown. Add the meat, tomato purée and half of the crushed garlic. Stir well and continue frying until the meat becomes brown. Then add 1 pint of water to the meat, followed by the mung beans, dill, salt and black pepper. Stir well and bring to the boil, then lower the heat, cover with a lid and cook gently for about one hour until the meat is tender. (If necessary add more water.)

While the meat is cooking, clean, wash and soak the rice.

When the meat is cooked, drain the rice and add it to the meat. Stir well, add the sweet pepper (if used), the 1⁄4 pint of water, cover with the lid, and turn the heat to low. Simmer the rice and meat slowly, stirring from time to time to prevent sticking, until the rice is soft and sticky and most of the water has been absorbed. Add more water if the rice becomes too dry. This takes about 30 minutes.

Take the rest of the garlic and fry it in the remaining tablespoon of oil until the colour changes. Add to the meat and rice mixture. Stir in the *char marsala*. Then place a thick clean cloth on top of the pan and cover with the lid. Leave the heat on low and cook slowly for another 30 minutes or so.

KETCHEREE QUROOT
A sticky rice and yoghurt dish   serves 4

A very popular dish. The *quroot* in its name is the dried yoghurt described on page 38; not easy to find or make, but the strained yoghurt or *chaka* used in this recipe is a good substitute.

8 oz (225 g) short grain rice
2 oz (50 g) mung beans (or
   green split peas)
salt
3 fl oz (75 ml) vegetable oil

15 fl oz (425 ml) strained
   yoghurt or *chaka* (p 38)
2 cloves of garlic, peeled
   and crushed
2 tsp dried mint
red pepper

Wash the rice and mung beans. Boil the latter in plenty of water until soft, then add the rice and enough water to cover by about 2″ (5 cm). Add the oil and a teaspoonful of salt, stir, bring to the boil, and cook gently over a medium low heat until the rice is soft and the water has evaporated (about ½-1 hour). Turn the heat to low and continue cooking for 20-30 minutes, stirring from time to time. The rice should have a thick, sticky consistency.

   While the rice is cooking, prepare either meatballs in a sauce (follow the recipe for *kofta chalau* on page 105, using 1 lb of minced meat and omitting the yoghurt) or meat *qorma* (see the recipe for *qorma chalau* at page 104).

   Combine the strained yoghurt with the garlic, a little salt, and a little red pepper.

   When all is ready, mound the rice on a large dish and shape it with the back of a spoon. Make a well in the top and fill this with the strained yoghurt, reserving some to serve separately. A little of the sauce from the meatballs or the *qorma* can be spooned over the rice. Finally, sprinkle with dried mint, and serve the meatballs or *qorma* separately.

Tabang wala

Vegetable Dishes and Salads

When I was in Afghanistan, bazaars were full of numerous cheap, good quality vegetables in season. Common vegetables include cauliflower, carrots, cabbage, turnips, marrows, spinach, potatoes, peas, lady's fingers (okra), leeks and French beans. These vegetables are usually added to a meat stew (*qorma*) and eaten with rice or *nan*. (If meat is not available a vegetable *qorma* is made.)

Onions are essential for many dishes. They are used in soups (*sherwa*), stews (*qorma*) and often in a *pilau*. They are also eaten raw in salads. *Gandana* is another important vegetable (p 40).

Tomatoes in season are plentiful and cheap. They are used to add colour and flavour to dishes, as well as being eaten raw in salads or just on their own with a little salt. Afghans make chutneys and purée from the cheap tomatoes in summer for use during the winter months. Aubergines and sweet peppers are cooked in several ways, and are essential for some special vegetable dishes such as *bonjon-e-buranee* and *dolma*.

Raw vegetables such as radishes, spring onions, cucumbers and lettuce are mainly eaten in salads or side dishes but are sometimes served as a quick snack with *nan*. A typical Afghan salad includes all these ingredients as well as tomatoes, and perhaps sweet peppers. There are no hard and fast rules about how to prepare a salad in Afghanistan, except that they are nearly always sprinkled with lemon or *norinj* (bitter orange) juice and left to marinate for about half an hour before serving. Vinegar is rarely used, and only very occasionally is olive or other oil added. Fresh coriander is often added to salads, either chopped up finely or left whole for garnishing. Mint is another herb often used to flavour or garnish salads. Sometimes hot green or red peppers are added.

Pulses are important in the Afghan diet as they often replace meat (see p 36). Red kidney beans, mung beans, chick peas, and split peas are the most common and are usually added to stews or soups.

DOLMA MURCH-E-SHIREEN
Stuffed peppers   serves 4

A dish which invites variations. The filling suggested can also be used to stuff tomatoes and aubergines, cabbage and vine leaves; the cooking time will vary, but it is always quick and simple to make and can be a meal in itself. If something more substantial is required it can be served with *chalau* or *pilau*.

4 oz (110 g) short or long grain rice
4 large green or red peppers
3 fl oz (75 ml) vegetable oil
1 lb (450 g) minced beef or lamb

2 medium onions, finely chopped
1 tsp ground coriander
salt and pepper

Wash the rice and soak it as usual.

Prepare the peppers by cutting off the stems end and scooping out the seeds.

Heat 2 fl oz of the oil in a pan and fry the meat and onions until they are brown. Turn down the heat and simmer for 10-15 minutes. Drain the rice and add to the meat mixture, then add the coriander, salt and pepper, and mix well. Fill the peppers with the meat mixture and fasten the tops of the peppers in place with cocktail sticks.

Place the prepared *dolma* in a deep pan. Add water so that it comes a third of the way up the *dolma*. Add the remaining 1 fl oz of oil and salt and pepper to taste. Bring to the boil, then reduce the heat and continue to boil, gently. Turn the *dolma* occasionally to ensure that they are evenly cooked. The cooking time is approximately 30-45 minutes.

Serve on a warm dish with some of the juices spooned over.

DOLMA BARG-E-KARAM
Stuffed cabbage leaves   serves 4

This can also be made with vine leaves. Cooking time will vary according to the freshness of the leaves.

4 oz (110 g) short or long grain rice	1 tsp ground coriander
3 fl oz (75 ml) vegetable oil	salt and pepper
1 lb (450 g) minced beef or lamb	8-12 cabbage leaves (or vine leaves)
2 medium onions, finely chopped	

Wash the rice and soak it as usual.

Prepare the meat filling as in the recipe for *Dolma murch-e-shireen* on the preceding page.

Remove the leaves from the head of a cabbage; the number you require depends on the size of the leaves. Drop the leaves into boiling salted water and boil for a couple of minutes. (If the main rib is too thick, cut it out.)

Put an amount of cooked filling appropriate to its size on each leaf. Form into sausage shapes by rolling up the leaves tightly and tucking in the ends. Lay the *dolma* in a single layer on the bottom of a pan. Add enough water or stock to cover, add the remaining 1 fl oz of oil, salt and pepper and cook gently, covered, for 25-30 minutes.

This dish improves with standing and can be cooked in advance and then reheated. Serve on a warmed dish with a little of the juice spooned over.

BONJON-E-BURANEE
Aubergines with yoghurt   serves 4

This delicious aubergine and yoghurt dish is particularly
popular with Afghans. We used to eat it on its own with freshly
baked *nan*, but it can be served with a *pilau* or *chalau*.

1 lb (450 g) aubergines	2 cloves of garlic,
8 fl oz (225 ml) vegetable oil	peeled and crushed
15 fl oz (425 ml) *chaka* (p 38)	2 tsp dried mint
or strained yoghurt	¼ tsp red pepper
4 oz (110 g) tomatoes	salt
1 medium onion, chopped	

Wash and peel the aubergines, slice them into rounds ¼-½"
(5 mm-1 cm) thick, spread them out on a board or plate,
sprinkle them with salt to draw out some of the water and any
bitterness, and allow to stand for 15-30 minutes. Rinse and then
wipe dry with a clean cloth or kitchen paper.

Heat the vegetable oil in a frying-pan and fry as many slices
of the aubergines as possible in one layer. Fry on both sides until
brown. Remove from the pan, shake off excess oil, and put to
one side. Repeat with the remaining aubergines, adding more
oil as necessary. (Aubergines soak up a lot of oil.)

Fry the chopped onions in the remaining oil until reddish-
brown. Slice the tomatoes. Arrange the aubergines, tomatoes
and onions in layers in a pan, sprinkling with a little salt and red
pepper. Add 2-3 tablespoons of water, cover the pan with a lid,
and simmer over a low heat for 40-50 minutes, adding a little
more water if necessary. The sauce should be thick, not watery.
Spoon off excess oil.

Meanwhile combine the strained yoghurt (or *chaka*), the
crushed garlic, a little salt and the dried mint.

Put half of the strained yoghurt on to a warm serving dish.
Carefully remove the aubergines from the pan with a fish slice,
and arrange them on the yoghurt. Top with the rest of the
yoghurt and any remaining sauce from the aubergines. Serve
immediately.

BURANEE KADU
Marrow with yoghurt   serves 4

This dish is a less rich alternative to *bonjon-e-buranee*.

15 fl oz (425 ml) *chaka* (p 38)   4 oz (110 g) tomatoes, sliced
  or strained yoghurt   or chopped
1 large marrow   salt
2 fl oz (55 ml) vegetable oil   red pepper
1 large onion, chopped

Peel the marrow and cut into 1″ (2.5 cm) rings. Scoop out the seeds. (The marrow can also be cut into 1″ (2.5 cm) cubes if preferred.)

Heat the oil in a large pan which has a lid, and fry the onion in it over a medium heat until soft and golden brown. Then add the marrow, fry it on both sides for a couple of minutes, and mix in the tomatoes, salt and pepper. Cover, turn the heat to low and cook for 30-40 minutes, or until the marrow is cooked and most of the liquid has evaporated. (Water will have come out of the marrow and tomatoes—it is not necessary to add any to this dish.)

To serve, put half of the yoghurt (*chaka*) on to a warmed dish and arrange the marrow on this. Top with the remaining yoghurt and any cooking juices left over. Serve immediately; suitable accompaniments are a rice dish or plain *nan*.

SABZI RAHWASH
Spinach with rhubarb   serves 4

Afghans often cook rhubarb and spinach together, an unusual and tasty vegetable dish which can be served with *chalau* or *pilau*, or with a *qorma* and fresh *nan*.

2 lb (900 g) spinach	2 tbs powdered dill weed
8 oz (450 g) leeks or	salt and pepper
gandana (p 40)	2 oz (50 g) rhubarb
4 fl oz (110 ml) vegetable oil	

Wash the spinach thoroughly, remove the stems and roughly chop up. Wash the leeks well and chop into small pieces.

Heat 3 fl oz of vegetable oil in a pan and fry the chopped leeks over a medium to high heat. When they are soft but not brown, add the spinach and stir continuously until the spinach reduces. Reduce the heat, cover, and continue to cook gently, stirring occasionally, until the oil comes to the surface. Then add the dill, salt and pepper. Add a little water if necessary.

While the spinach is cooking, skin and wash the rhubarb and cut it into 1″ (2.5 cm) lengths. Fry it briefly in the remaining 1 fl oz of oil over a medium heat, without letting it brown, then add it to the spinach and cook for a further half an hour or until it is sufficiently cooked.

QORMA-E-SHAST-E-ARUS or BOMYA
Okra stew   serves 4

Shast-e-arus in Dari means bride's finger.

1 lb (450 g) okra (lady's fingers)	1 oz (25 g) split peas
use young, small ones	8 oz (225 g) tomatoes,
3 fl oz (75 ml) vegetable oil	skinned and chopped
1 medium onion, chopped	salt and pepper
	1 tsp powdered dill weed

Clean the okra and cut off the stalks.

Heat the oil in a pan and fry the chopped onion until brown. Add the okra and fry gently, stirring carefully until they are well coated with the oil. Add the split peas, tomatoes, salt and pepper, stir and mix the ingredients, and then cook over a medium heat for a few minutes. Next, add just enough water to cover the okra, and the dill. Bring back to the boil, then turn down the heat and simmer for 30-45 minutes or until the liquid has reduced, the sauce has thickened, and the oil has come to the surface.

This *qorma* is usually served with *chalau*, although it can be served with a *pilau*.

DAL
Moong dal stew   serves 4

Dal is an economical dish, similar to the Indian dish of the same name, and eaten with *chalau* or *yakhni pilau*. Sometimes minced meat is served with the rice and *dal*, but never a meat *qorma*.

8 oz (225 g) moong dal (p 37)	3 tbs vegetable oil
1 medium onion, chopped	½ tsp ground ginger
1-2 cloves of garlic,	½ tsp turmeric
peeled and crushed	1-2 tsp tomato purée
	salt and pepper

Wash the *dal* in cold water, drain, put into a pan with enough water to cover it by about 2″ (5 cm), and bring to the boil. Remove any surface scum, then cover (but leave the lid slightly ajar), turn the heat to low and simmer for about half an hour. Stir often to prevent sticking.

Fry the chopped onion and half of the crushed garlic in 2 tablespoons of the oil until lightly browned. Add the ginger, turmeric and tomato purée. Stir and fry for a minute or two then add these ingredients to the *dal* together with more water so that the level is 1″ (2.5 cm) above the *dal*. Season with salt and pepper, and simmer until the water has evaporated and the *dal* is well cooked; thick but runny. This takes about an hour.

Just before serving fry the remaining garlic in the remaining 1 tablespoon of oil and pour over the *dal*.

SALATA BONJON-E-RHUMI-E-PIAZ
Tomato and onion salad   serves 4-6

This is often prepared as a side dish to go with rice dishes or kebabs. It is also eaten as a snack with fresh *nan*. Some Afghans add hot green peppers and finely chop all the ingredients.

1 medium onion, finely sliced	1 lb (450 g) tomatoes, thinly sliced
salt	
1-2 cloves of garlic, peeled and crushed	3 tbs fresh coriander leaves, finely chopped (reserve a few sprigs for garnishing)
juice of half a lemon	

Place the finely sliced onions in a bowl and add about 1 teaspoon of salt. Mix well, then rinse in water and drain.

Add the crushed garlic and a little salt to the lemon juice.

Mix the sliced tomatoes and onions together with the finely chopped coriander. Add the lemon juice and garlic and leave to marinate in a cool place for about 30 minutes.

Serve on a flat dish or in a bowl, garnished with sprigs of coriander.

Pickles and Chutneys

Pickles and chutneys, *turshi* and *chutni*, are an essential part of Afghan food. Rarely is a meal served without one homemade speciality. Pickles are made from baby aubergines, carrots, beans, chillies, small onions, limes or lemons and marrow. Afghans make their own tomato, peach or apricot and coriander chutneys.

TURSHI LIMO
Lemon pickle

There are many recipes for the traditional lemon pickle, of which I give two. It is usually made with the very small lemons or limes which are readily available in Afghanistan, but ordinary lemons can be used in the first recipe.

RECIPE ONE   makes about 2 one pound jars

1 lb (450 g) lemons or limes   ½ tbs fenugreek
½ tbs black cumin seeds   ½ tbs sugar
  (*kalonji*)   1 tbs salt

Cut the lemons in half, squeeze out and reserve the juice. Scoop out the insides and, if the lemons are large, cut the halves into two. Put them into salted water for 24 hours.

Take the lemon peels from the water and boil as many times as necessary in fresh, clean water to remove all bitterness and make them soft. Drain, then boil them again, this time in the lemon juice, for a couple of minutes. Add the rest of the ingredients, leave to cool, then place in clean, dry jars and screw on lids ready to store. The lemon peels should always be covered by lemon juice in the jars, so add extra lemon juice if required.

RECIPE TWO

2 lb (900 g) very small lemons or limes	1 tbs sugar
	2 tbs salt
1 tbs black cumin seed (*kalonji*)	
1 tbs fenugreek	

Squeeze out the juice from half of the lemons and reserve. Puncture holes in the skins of the remaining lemons before putting inside clean, dry jars. Add the lemon juice and the other ingredients. If the lemons are not covered by juice, add more lemon juice and proportionately more sugar. Screw on the lids and leave in a warm and preferably sunny place until the lemons become soft and are no longer bitter. How long this takes depends upon where the jars are placed. If the juice evaporates, add more lemon juice.

TURSHI ZARDAK
Carrot pickle

This pickle has been adapted so that canned carrots may be used. The taste of the vinegar may be too strong for some people; it can be diluted by using a little water or liquid from the can of carrots.

1 hot green pepper	½ tsp black cumin seeds (*kalonji*)
7 oz (200 g) can of small, young carrots	1 clove of garlic, peeled and crushed
vinegar	
½ tsp salt	2 tsp sugar

Boil the hot green pepper in a little water for 5 to 10 minutes until soft, then chop it into small pieces.

Drain off the liquid from the can of carrots. Put the carrots in a pan and add just enough vinegar to cover them. Boil for a couple of minutes. Add the black cumin seed, salt, crushed garlic, sugar and the hot green pepper. Mix well and put into a clean, dry jar, adding more vinegar if necessary in order to cover the carrots. Screw on the lid and leave for a few days.

CHUTNI SHAFTALU / ZARDALU
Peach or Apricot chutney   makes 2 one pound jars

This recipe has been adapted so that canned peaches or apricots may be used.

1 can (1 lb 13 oz: 820 g) peaches or apricots	9 fl oz (250 ml) white wine vinegar
1-2 hot green peppers, seeds removed and finely chopped	1 tsp black cumin seed (*kalonji*) 1 tbs ground ginger 1 tbs salt

Drain the peaches, mash them with a fork, and combine with the green pepper. Boil the vinegar for 5 minutes, then add to it the black cumin seeds, ginger, salt and (if wished) a little of the syrup from the peaches. Remove the vinegar from the heat and add the peaches and pepper. When cool, place in clean dry jars with tightly fitting lids. Store in a cool place or in a refrigerator.

CHUTNI GASHNEETCH
Coriander chutney   makes about a 1 lb jar

This chutney has a sharp taste and is rich in vitamins A and C. Small amounts are served with main meals. It keeps well in a refrigerator.

8 oz (225 g) fresh coriander (not the lower stems or roots)	1 oz (25 g) walnuts 1 oz (25 g) sugar 8 fl oz (225 ml) lemon juice or white wine vinegar
½-1 oz (10-25 g) hot green pepper (with seeds removed)	1-1½ tbs salt
½-1 oz (10-25 g) garlic, peeled	1 oz (25 g) raisins (optional)

Grind the coriander, green pepper, garlic and walnuts, making sure that they are mixed thoroughly. Add the sugar to the lemon juice or vinegar and again mix well. Add this to the coriander mixture, with the salt and raisins, mix again, put into a clean jar (or jars), screw on the lid and store in the refrigerator.

Fruits, Desserts and Sweet Pastries

Desserts and pastries are considered a luxury and are usually made for weddings, feast days, *Eid* and other special occasions. Some of them are quick and easy but some require time and effort, and a trial run. Cakes and biscuits are rarely prepared in the home as few families have facilities for baking. More often, they are bought from local bakeries called *kulcha feroshee*. However, this lack of cakes is more than made up for by the variety of fruit available. Fruit is often the only dessert. Large bowls are filled with: grapes, peaches, apples, oranges, bananas, plums, nectarines, pears, pomegranates, apricots, tangerines, satsumas, cherries, strawberries, melon and water melon.

The fruit offered after a meal obviously depends on the time of year and what is in season. Melon and grapes are perhaps most abundant in summer and there are numerous varieties of both. Many of the grapes are made into the green and red raisins for which Afghanistan is famous. The green have the best flavour and are also the more expensive. Raisins, apart from being used in some Afghan dishes, are eaten alone or mixed with nuts and served with tea, especially for guests.

Mulberry and walnut trees are found mainly in northern Afghanistan. In the winter, when fruit and vegetables are scarce and expensive, a preparation of ground, dried mulberry and walnut, called *chakidah*, helps supplement a somewhat deficient diet. Travellers often carry dried fruit and nut combinations tied in the end of their turban cloths. Other nuts found in Afghanistan include pistachios from the Herat region, and almonds and pine nuts. Apricot kernels are often substituted for almonds. Nuts are used in *pilau*, desserts and pastries. Almonds coated with a sugar syrup are called *noql*.

When a recipe in this chapter calls for pistachio nuts or almonds, unsalted ones are meant. When saffron, which is expensive, figures as an ingredient, you can do as many Afghans do and substitute some cheaper yellow colouring.

MIWA NAUROZEE
New Year fruit compote serves 6-8

Miwa means fruit, and *Naurozee* the New Year. As one would
expect, this compote is made for New Year celebrations. The
original version was made with seven fruits, each of which had
a name including the letter *seen*. So the dish may also be called
Haft (seven) *seen* or *Haft miwa*.

The seven fruits were: *khastah*, apricot kernels; *pistah*, pistachio
nuts; *kishmish surkh*, red raisins; *kishmish sabz*, green raisins;
kishmish sia (sometimes called *monaqa*), large black raisins with
seeds; *saib*, apple; and *sinjed*. *Sinjed* is the fruit of a tree of the
genus *Elaeagnus* in the oleaster family. It is related to the North
American silverberry. It looks like a very small date, but is
redder, with a large stone, a bland flavour and a mealy texture.

Tradition requires that, before *Haft seen* is served, it is blessed
by the reading of seven passages from the *Qo'ran*, called *Haft
Salaam*. These passages are special prayers to bring health.

The ingredients now used to make *Miwa Naurozee* vary from
family to family. Many use the small, sweet, dried white apricots
called *shakar paura*. Almonds (*badom*) often replace apricot
kernels, and walnuts (*charmaz*) are a common addition. It is
fortunate that the recipe is flexible, since it can easily be made
with whatever dried fruits and nuts are readily available, as in
this version.

4 oz (110 g) dried apricots	2 oz (50 g) pistachio nuts
4 oz (110 g) dark seedless raisins	2 oz (50 g) almonds
2 oz (50 g) light raisins	2 oz (50 g) cherries
2 oz (50 g) walnuts	

Wash the apricots and both types of raisins and place in a bowl.
Cover with cold water to 2" (5 cm) above the fruit. Cover and set
aside for two days.

Put the walnuts, pistachios and almonds in another bowl or
pan and add boiling water. Leave to soak, then peel off all the
skins as they soften. This is a fiddly job, especially with the
walnuts, but it is well worth the effort. Throw away the water.

After the apricots and raisins have been soaked for two days, combine the fruits and the juice they have been soaking in with the nuts and add the cherries.

To serve, spoon the fruit and nuts, well mixed, and some juice into individual dishes or cups.

If this dish is left for a couple of days in the refrigerator the juice will become sweeter.

FIRNI
Afghan custard   serves 6-8

One of the traditional desserts, often made for special occasions, such as wedding parties and *Eid*. It is simple and quick.

1¾ pint (1 litre) milk	1 oz (25 g) finely chopped or
10 oz (275 g) sugar	ground pistachio
2 oz (50 g) cornflour	1 oz (25 g) finely chopped or
½ tsp ground green or	ground almond
white cardamom seeds	

Mix the cornflour with a small amount of water into a paste.

Heat the milk in a pan and, when hot but not boiling, add the sugar. (More or less sugar may be used, according to taste). Stir well. When the milk is close to boiling, slowly add the cornflour paste to the mixture, stirring continuously. Bring to the boil, add the cardamom, turn down the heat and simmer for about 5 minutes, stirring occasionally.

Pour the *firni* on to a shallow serving dish and decorate it with finely chopped or ground pistachio and almond.

Firni is always eaten cold.

MAUGHOOT
Afghan jelly   serves 6-8

This is made in the same way as *firni*, except that water is used instead of milk and it is flavoured and coloured with saffron.

13⁄4 pint (1 litre) water
10 oz (275 g) sugar
2 oz (50 g) cornflour
1⁄4 tsp ground green or
   white cardamom seeds

1⁄4-1⁄2 tsp saffron
1 oz (25 g) flaked or finely
   chopped pistachio
1 oz (25 g) flaked or finely
   chopped almond

Mix the cornflour with a little water to form a paste.

Heat the water and when hot, but not boiling, add the sugar. (More or less sugar may be used, according to taste.) Stir well. When the water is close to boiling, slowly add the cornflour paste to the liquid, stirring continuously. Bring to the boil and add the cardamom and saffron. Turn down the heat and boil gently for 2-5 minutes until the liquid becomes clear. Remove from the heat and pour on to a shallow serving dish. It should flatten out completely. Sprinkle on to it, as decoration, the pistachio and almond.

Maughoot, like *firni*, is always eaten cold.

SHEER BIRINJ
Milky rice pudding   serves 4-6

A short grain rice dish similar to English milky rice puddings and not thick and sticky like *shola* or *daygcha*.

4 oz (110 g) short grain rice
1 pint (570 ml) water
18 fl oz (500 ml) milk
4 oz (110 g) sugar
2 tsp rose-water

1⁄4 tsp ground green or white
   cardamom seeds
1 oz (25 g) finely chopped or
   ground pistachio
   or almond

Put the washed rice in a pan, add the water, bring to the boil, then turn down the heat to medium and boil gently until the rice is cooked and soft and all the water has evaporated. Stir from time to time to prevent the rice from sticking. Add the milk and bring back to the boil, then turn down the heat again and boil gently until the mixture thickens a little bit, then add the sugar. Continue to boil gently, stirring often to prevent sticking, until the sugar has dissolved and the mixture has thickened, although still runny. Add the ground cardamom and the rose-water and cook for another 1-2 minutes.

Serve the rice on a large flat plate, decorated with the ground pistachio or almond. Afghans serve this dish cold, but it can be eaten warm, if preferred.

DAYGCHA
Sweet, sticky rice pudding   serves 6-8

Daygcha is a thick and sticky rice dish often prepared for special ceremonies. It is cooked on the final Wednesday of the lunar month *Safar* and also for an *Eid* and birthdays. Sometimes it is served with evening tea.

16 fl oz (450 ml) water	16 fl oz (450 ml) milk
8 oz (225 g) short grain rice	8 fl oz (225 g) sugar
4 oz (110 g) butter or margarine	½ tsp ground green or white
(preferably unsalted)	cardamom seeds
pinch of salt	

Bring the water to the boil in a pan and add the salt, the rice and the butter or margarine. Boil gently, until the rice is soft. Stir occasionally during the cooking. You may have to add more water but all water should have been absorbed by the end of it. Add the milk, sugar, cardamom and simmer until all the liquid evaporates and the rice is thick. Stir frequently to prevent the rice from sticking to the bottom of the pan.

Cover the pan with a cloth and then a tightly fitting lid, and leave to cook slowly over a low heat for 20-30 minutes. Or, better, put it in a covered casserole into a preheated oven at 150°C (300°F, mark 2) for the same length of time.

To serve, remove the rice to a large dish and let it cool for about one hour.

SHOLA SHIREEN
Sweet rice with nuts serves 4-6

This moist rice dish is often prepared in the lunar month of *Muharram*, for *Nauroz*, for *Eid* and for *Nazer* (see pp 18 ff).

8 oz (225 g) white short grain
    rice
2 fl oz (55 ml) milk
6 oz (175 g) sugar
¼ tsp saffron
1 tbs rose-water

½ tsp ground green or
    white cardamom seeds
1 oz (25 g) pistachio,
    skinned and chopped
1 oz (25 g) almond, skinned
    and chopped

Rinse the rice in cold water, drain it, put it into pan and add enough water to cover it by about 2″ (5 cm). Bring to the boil, cover with a lid, reduce the heat and boil gently, stirring frequently to prevent sticking, until the rice softens and the water has evaporated. (This takes approximately 20-30 minutes.)

Add the milk, sugar and saffron. Reduce the heat to low and cover with the lid. Simmer for another 20-30 minutes until the rice is well cooked and soft. Add the rose-water, ground cardamom, pistachio and almond. Stir well and simmer for a few more minutes. Place on a large flat dish. Serve cold.

SHOLA-E-OLBA
Sweet rice with fenugreek serves 4-6

8 oz (225 g) white short grain
    rice
3 oz (75 g) butter or margarine
½ oz (10 g) fenugreek

½ tsp saffron
6 oz (175 g) brown sugar

Wash the rice in cold water and drain.

Heat the butter or margarine in a pan and add the fenugreek. Stir until brown, but be careful not to burn it. Add the rice and stir well. Add enough water to cover the rice by about 2″ (5 cm), and the saffron. Boil gently until the rice is soft. You may have to add more water during the cooking, but by the end it should all have been absorbed. Add the sugar, stir again, reduce the heat and simmer for half an hour. Serve either warm or cold.

HALWA-E-AURDI
Wheat halva   serves 6-8

There are many recipes and variations of *halwa*. The *halwa* prepared in Afghanistan is closely related to other wheat desserts which are popular throughout the Near East, Central Asia and India. *Halwa* is a traditional dish served at most festive celebrations and it is also made for *Nazer* (p 22). It is mildy sweet and delicately flavoured. Nuts are added to the finest *halwa*, as in this recipe, but it is often made without them.

6 oz (175 g) margarine or vegetable fat
8 oz (225 g) *chappatti* or wheatmeal flour
6 oz (175 g) sugar
15 fl oz (425 ml) water

1 oz (25 g) pistachio, flaked
1 oz (25 g) almond, flaked
½ tsp ground green or white cardamom seeds
½ tsp rose-water (optional)

Mix the sugar with half of the water.

Melt the fat over a medium to high heat, add the flour slowly, and stir and fry until it turns a golden colour. Next, add the sugar and water mixture to the flour and fat mixture, stirring continuously; then add the rest of the water and mix gently with a spoon. The fat will separate. Continue cooking until the water has evaporated, at which point the pistachio, almond, cardamom, and rose-water (if used) are put in. Cover with a lid and put into a preheated oven at 150°C (300°F, mark 2) for half an hour.

Serve *halwa* slightly warm, or cold, in a large dish or bowl, or in individual dessert dishes.

HALWA-E-AURD-E-BIRINJI
Ground rice halva

This *halwa* is made in exactly the same way as *halwa-e-aurdi*, except that ground rice replaces the flour. Also, rose-water is more commonly used in flavouring; and the amount should be increased to 1 teaspoon. *Halwa-e-aurd-e-birinji* has a finer and more delicate flavour and texture than ordinary *halwa-e-aurdi*.

HALWA-E-AURD-E-SUJEE
Semolina halva

This is the same *halwa* as *halwa-e-aurdi* and *halwa-e-aurd-e-birinji* (p 133) except that it is made with semolina, and not flour.

HALWA SWANAK
Nut brittle   makes 5 or 6

A kind of hard toffee, usually made for special occasions such as an *Eid*. Afghans usually make quite large *halwa swanak* but any size can be made. This recipe, given to me by my sister-in-law, is for small ones, which are easier to prepare.

2 oz (50 g) sugar
1 fl oz (25 ml) vegetable oil
1 oz (25 g) plain white flour

1 oz (25 g) walnuts or pistachio, ground or finely chopped

Put the sugar in a pan over a medium to high heat. Stir vigorously until it melts and turns golden brown, and a froth appears on top of it. Then carefully add the oil, stirring vigorously as you do so. Turn down the heat to low and add the flour, a little at a time, stirring quickly all the time. Add the chopped nuts. Continue stirring for one minute. Then, using a warmed tablespoon, remove a spoonful of the mixture. If it is still too hot to handle, wait a minute or so until it has cooled down a bit, then form it into a round ball. Work quickly as, if the mixture cools down too much, it will be difficult to mould. Flatten the ball and roll out into a round shape to a thickness of about 1/8"(2.5 mm). Repeat until all the mixture has been used up. Leave to cool.

HALWA-E-ZARDAK
Carrot halva   serves 3-4

1 lb (450 g) carrots
4 fl oz (110 ml) vegetable oil
3/4 pint (425 ml) milk
4 oz (110 g) sugar
1 oz (25 g) pistachio, chopped into quarters

1 oz (25 g) almond, chopped into quarters
1 oz (25 g) sultanas or raisins
1/2 tsp ground green or white cardamom seeds

Shred or grate the carrots and drain off any liquid. Heat the oil, reserving 1 tablespoon, and stir the shredded carrots in it until they begin to brown and any water has evaporated. Add the milk and sugar, stir well, then reduce the heat and simmer for about an hour, stirring occasionally. All the liquid should have evaporated and the oil will have separated, coming to the surface.

Fry the nuts and sultanas in the remaining tablespoon of oil until they are lightly browned and the sultanas have swollen up. Add to the cooked carrot. Add the ground cardamom. Mix well and leave for a further 2 minutes or so on a low heat.

SAMBOSA SHIREEN
Sweet stuffed pastry makes 24 plus

Afghans like to make a sweet variation of *sambosa*. This is the same recipe as for *sambosa goshti* (p 69), except that the pastry squares are filled with *halwa-e-aurd-e-sujee* or *halwa-e-aurd-e-birinji*.

1 lb (450 g) frozen puff pastry
  or *sambosa* dough made with
  1 lb flour (p 68)
halwa made with 8 oz (225 g)
  semolina or rice flour

icing sugar, sifted
½-1 oz (10-25 g) ground
  pistachio (optional)
vegetable oil for deep-frying

Prepare the *halwa*.

Roll out the pastry as thinly as possible and cut into 4" (10 cm) squares. Place 1-2 tablespoons of the *halwa* on each square. Fold the squares to make triangles and seal the edges tightly.

Having heated enough vegetable oil in a frying-pan, deep-fry the *sambosa* until golden brown on both sides. Remove from the oil and drain. Dust the warm pastries with a little icing sugar and ground pistachio if used.

These *sambosa* are usually served with tea, either hot or cold.

NAN-E-PARATA
Sweet fried bread   makes 4

½ oz (10 g) dried yeast
10 fl oz (275 ml) lukewarm
    water
1¼ lb (560 g) plain white
    flour, sifted

1½ tsp salt
12 tbs oil, plus more for
    deep-frying
2 oz (50 g) icing sugar

Mix the yeast and water together and leave to soften. Sift the flour with the salt, then add the yeast mixture gradually to this (with more water if necessary) and mix to form a firm dough. Knead the dough until it is smooth and elastic, shape it into a ball and leave it, covered, in a bowl for about half an hour.

Divide the dough into four balls, and again divide each of these into four, making sixteen altogether.

On a lightly floured board roll each ball in turn into a disc no thicker than 1/16″ (1.5 mm). Then, using a pastry brush, brush 1 tablespoon of oil over three discs and stack them on top of each other, topping with a fourth. Press down lightly with a rolling pin. Each stack should not be more than ¼″ (5 mm) thick. Repeat, making four breads in all.

Heat enough vegetable oil in a large frying-pan and deep-fry the breads over a medium to high heat, one at a time, until light brown. They should not be too crisp. Remove and drain. Sift the icing sugar over the hot breads, on both sides.

Smaller breads can be made, but this size is traditional.

GOASH-E-FEEL
Elephant's ear pastry   makes 8

Elephant's ear is the literal meaning of *goash-e-feel*, a name given because of the shape and size of these crisp, bubbly, sweet pastries. They are usually served with tea; and often a bride's family sends them to the bride and groom the day after the wedding. They are also made for *Nauroz* (New Year's Day, 21 March, the first day of spring).

For best results, the pastry must be rolled out paper thin, and the oil for frying must be very hot.

1 egg

milk

8 oz (225 g) plain white flour

salt

vegetable oil for frying

2 oz (50 g) icing sugar

2 oz (50 g) ground pistachio

Break the egg into a bowl, beat it, and add enough milk to make the liquid up to 8 fl oz (225 ml). Sift the flour with a pinch of salt, add it to the egg and milk mixture, and mix well to form a firm dough. Knead on a lightly floured board for about 10 minutes until smooth and elastic. Divide the dough into eight equal balls, cover with a moistened cloth and set to one side in a cool place for about half an hour.

On a lightly floured board, roll out each of the eight balls until paper thin; they should be approximately 7″ (18 cm) in diameter. Shape the 'ears' by pleating one side of each round piece of dough. Nip together with wet fingers, to prevent the pleats from opening during drying.

In a frying-pan of similar diameter, heat enough oil to shallow-fry the pastries. When the oil is very hot, put in the 'ears' one at a time and fry until golden brown and bubbly, then turn and fry the other side until golden brown. As you remove the pastries from the pan, shake off the excess oil gently, then sprinkle them on both sides with a mixture of sifted icing sugar and ground pistachio.

There are many variations of *goash-e-feel*, so do not feel limited as to the size and shapes you can make. Some Afghans make what is called *goash-e-asp* (horse's ear), or bow knots. Sizes vary considerably.

QATLAMA
makes approximately 6

A sweet fried pastry, more common in northern Afghanistan, which can be a bit fiddly to make. This recipe gives the traditional way of making *qatlama*. However, smaller shapes — triangular, square or diamond — can be made and five or six layers of pastry instead of seven can be used.

2 eggs
1 lb (450 g) plain white flour
pinch salt
½ tsp baking powder
2 tbs melted margarine or
vegetable oil

4 fl oz (110 ml) milk or water
4 tbs vegetable oil, and
more for deep-frying
2 oz (50 g) icing sugar
2 oz (50 g) ground pistachio

Beat the eggs in a mixing bowl until they foam.

Sift the flour, salt and baking powder together into a large mixing bowl. Make a well and add the egg and melted margarine. Gradually add the milk or water (more or less, as needed) and mix to form a stiff dough. Knead for about 5-10 minutes until the dough is firm and elastic. Shape the dough into a ball, cover the bowl with a cloth and leave to stand for about half an hour.

Divide the dough into four balls, then roll each out, on a lightly floured board, as thinly as possible: aim for a diameter of about 14″ (32 cm). Cut each into 4″ (10 cm) squares. Oil each square with a pastry brush and put the squares one on top of the other in piles of seven. Fold each seven-layered pile into a triangle, and press down gently with a rolling pin.

In a deep pan, heat enough oil for deep-frying and fry the pastries until golden brown. Remove from the oil and while still hot sprinkle with a mixture of sifted icing sugar and ground pistachio. Serve warm or cold.

KHAJOOR or BOSRAUQ
Afghan doughnuts
makes about 50

The shape of these small fried cakes varies from family to family. When made in the traditional way, *khajoor* are pressed over a wire strainer or sieve which gives a mesh-like imprint.

Many people do not caramelise the sugar, as in this recipe, but add it directly to the mixture of flour and salt.

4 fl oz (110 ml) warm water	4 fl oz (110 ml) vegetable oil
½ tbs dried yeast	or margarine
1 lb 3 oz (525 g) plain white	8 oz (225 g) sugar
flour	4 tbs more water
½ tsp salt	vegetable oil for frying

Combine the yeast with the warm water and set aside to soften.

Sift the flour and salt together in a large mixing bowl.

In a pan, melt the sugar and oil together. Pour quickly into the flour and stir rapidly to prevent the formation of large sugar crystals as the caramelised sugar cools. Then add the yeast mixture and the 4 tablespoons of cold water to make a firm dough. Do not allow it to stand, but at once take a little of the mixture and form it into a ball about the size of an egg. Flatten this against the convex surface of a sieve to a thickness of about ⅛" (3 mm) and a diameter of about 2" (5 cm), then roll it up loosely and seal (see the drawing).

Fry the cakes in deep oil or fat until golden brown, remove, drain well and cool.

BAQLAWA
Sweet pastry with nuts makes about 30

This dessert, which is similar to the *baqlawa* of other parts of Asia and central Europe, is rich and requires a lot of preparation. For quickness, Greek filo pastry, readily available in many delicatessens and supermarkets, can be used.

2 egg yolks	7 oz (200 g) ground walnuts
8 fl oz (220 ml) water	4 oz (110 g) ground pistachio
1 lb (450 g) plain white flour	
2 oz (50 g) cornflour, and some	*for the syrup*
more for rolling out pastry	1 lb (450 g) sugar
1 tsp baking powder	8 fl oz (220 ml) more water
¼ tsp salt	¼ tsp saffron
2 oz (50 g) margarine	½ tsp ground white or green
8 fl oz (225 ml) vegetable oil	cardamom seeds

Mix the egg yolks with 4 fl oz (110 ml) of the water. Sift the flour, cornflour, baking powder and salt into a large mixing bowl. Rub in the margarine. Add the egg yolks and mix with the hand, gradually adding the other 4 fl oz of water (and a little more, if necessary) until a firm dough is made. Knead the dough until smooth and elastic, then divide and shape it into twelve equal balls. Oil each ball with some of the vegetable oil and set aside for about 20 minutes.

Prepare a baking tray approximately 20″ by 14″ by 2″ (50 by 35 by 5 cm) by oiling generously.

On a board lightly dusted with cornflour, roll out each ball of dough until paper thin and of a size which will fit the baking tray. Brush three of these sheets of dough with oil, and lay them on top of each other, then sprinkle the top layer with about a third of the ground walnuts and a quarter of the ground pistachio. Repeat this whole process twice, so that you have three triple-layered piles. Oil the last three sheets of pastry and place one on top of each pile, brushing the top with any remaining oil.

Using a sharp knife, cut carefully through all the layers lengthwise to form strips about 1½″ (4 cm) wide; then cut diagonally across these to form diamond-shaped pieces. Put these in a preheated oven at 180°C (350°F, mark 4) for 35-45 minutes or until the pastry is set and golden brown on top.

Just before the pastry is ready to come out of the oven, prepare a syrup. Put the sugar and water, saffron and cardamom in a pan over a high heat, bring to the boil, and boil until the syrup thickens (4-5 minutes). Keep the syrup warm until the pastry is brought out of the oven. Spoon the syrup over the warm pastry until all of it is used and the pastry is well covered. Sprinkle the reserved pistachio on top and then leave to cool for about three hours before serving.

JELABI

Jelabi are usually eaten as a sweet in winter after eating fish. It was a common sight in winter for us to see the fish in the bazaars displayed alongside mountains of *jelabi*. *Jelabi* are prepared for engaged couples and by tradition the groom's family send them with fish to the bride's family on New Year's Day.

Jelabi are difficult to make and I have to confess that I have not been successful in making them in perfect shapes. The recipe has been given to me by my sister-in-law, who makes them without any problem. She tells me that the secret lies in the oil being very hot and a steady, firm and confident hand in squeezing out the batter into the oil.

	for the syrup:
1 level tbs baking powder	
10 fl oz (275 ml) warm water	8 oz (225 g) sugar
1 level tbs yoghurt	8 fl oz (225 ml) water
8 oz (225 g) plain flour	pinch of saffron or turmeric
oil for deep-frying	few drops of rose-water

Add the baking powder to 4 tablespoons of the warm water and mix. Add the yoghurt and then leave in the oven, preheated to its lowest setting, for about 15 minutes.

Make a thick batter by beating the flour and the remaining 8 fl oz of warm water. Add the yoghurt mixture. Cover with a thick, clean cloth and leave the batter to rise in a warm place for about 1-2 hours.

Dissolve the sugar in the 8 fl oz of water, add a pinch of saffron (or turmeric) and a few drops of rose-water. Boil over a high heat until the syrup thickens (about 5-6 minutes). Remove from the heat but keep warm in a bowl over a pan of hot water.

In a pan, heat to very hot enough oil for deep-frying. Pour the batter into a piping bag fitted with a fine nozzle and pipe straight on to the very hot oil a spiral of three circles and then form two straight lines across. This has to be done very quickly and may need practice. Fry until golden brown, then remove from the oil carefully with tongs or a perforated spoon and dip into the warm syrup, coating both sides. Leave to cool on a separate tray dish. Repeat until all the batter is used up.

Making jelabi

SHEER PAYRA
Milk and sugar sweet

This rich sweet is served with tea on special occasions such as the birth of a baby.

1 lb (450 g) sugar
5 fl oz (150 ml) water
8 oz (225 g) powdered milk
1 oz (25 g) walnuts, finely chopped

¼-½ tsp ground white or green cardamom seeds
½ oz (15 g) ground or finely chopped pistachio

Grease or oil a baking tin or dish which is approximately 7" by 9" (18 by 23 cm) and 1½" (4 cm) deep.

Mix the sugar with the water in a pan, stir over a high heat until dissolved, then boil for 1-2 minutes until syrupy (the 'smooth' stage, when a little of the syrup placed on a cold saucer will not run but becomes white and congealed). When this stage is reached, quickly remove from the heat and add the powdered milk, slowly and mixing well. The mixture will thicken. Stir in the walnuts and ground cardamom.

Put the mixture immediately into the prepared tin or dish. Sprinkle with pistachio and leave to cool and set slightly. Cut the mixture into diamond or square shapes of about 1½" by 1½" (4 by 4 cm) with a greased, sharp knife. Leave to set for 2 hours in a cool place or refrigerator.

ABRASHUM KEBAB
'Silk kebab'   makes about 9-12

An ancient dish, which is usually only made for festive occasions such as weddings. It is really a sort of sweet omelette, but cooked in an extraordinary way so that, as the name implies, the finished products seem to be made of silken threads. Preparation is difficult, and varies from family to family. I have used the method which my sister-in-law taught me. As will be clear from the recipe, the quantity made will depend on the size of frying-pan used.

5 eggs	1 oz (25 g) ground pistachio
7 oz (200 g) sugar	pinch of saffron (optional)
½ pint (275 ml) water	½-¾ pint (275-425 ml)
½ tsp ground white or	vegetable oil for frying
green cardamom seeds	

Whisk the eggs in a bowl until smooth but not frothy.

Add the sugar to the water in a pan and bring to the boil. The sugar will dissolve. Boil until syrupy for about 5 minutes. Add the ground cardamom and saffron, if used. Keep warm over a low heat.

Heat the vegetable oil until hot in a large deep frying-pan.

The next procedure may need a little practice. The hand should be put well down into the egg mixture until it is coated with egg. With widespread fingers, palm down, scoop up some of the egg mixture. Then rapidly string the egg across the hot fat making a mesh of 'silk' threads and covering the surface of the oil like a piece of fabric. The finer the threads, the better. Dip the hand into the egg again and repeat the process until the oil is covered with a fine mesh of egg mixture. Do this as fast as possible. The egg will become a golden colour in the oil quite quickly. Take a skewer and loosen the 'threads' round the edge of the pan. Then, using two skewers and starting at one edge of the pan, hold one skewer on top of the threads and the other underneath, lift up the threads from the oil and by turning the skewers round each other, roll up the threads loosely to form a roll about 1″ (2.5 cm) in diameter. Take the skewers with the kebab rolled around them away from the frying-pan. Carefully detach the kebab and place it on a dish. Spoon about 2-3 table-spoons of the prepared, warm syrup over the kebab and sprinkle with ground pistachio, and more cardamom if wished. Repeat until all the egg mixture has been used up. Serve cold, with tea. If you like, cut up each kebab into two or three portions. They will, by the way, keep in the refrigerator for several days without loss of quality.

NOQL-E-BADOMI
Sugared almonds

These are sweets to be served with tea. They are not easy to make, and Afghans usually buy them from the bazaar to save themselves the trouble.

It is very important to prepare the syrup correctly and, when coating the almonds, to shake the pan vigorously. If the syrup is boiled for too long, the almonds will stick together; if not boiled for long enough, it will not become white. The coating will not be smooth, as with commercial sugared almonds, but uneven and bubbly.

1 lb (450 g) almonds
1 lb (450 g) sugar
¼ pint (150 ml) water

½-1 tsp ground white or
green cardamom seeds

First of all roast the almonds in a preheated oven at 150°C (300°F, mark 2).

While the almonds are roasting, warm the water in a pan. Add the sugar and cardamom to the warm water, dissolve the sugar over a medium to high heat, then boil for a couple of minutes until syrupy (the 'smooth' stage, when a little of the syrup, put on a cold saucer, does not run but becomes white and congealed). At this point, reduce the heat. Meanwhile you have put half of the almonds in a large pan. Taking one spoonful of the syrup at a time, pour it over the almonds and shake the pan vigorously in order to coat the almonds completely. Continue until all the almonds in the pan are covered and white, then repeat with the remaining almonds.

KULCHA NAUROZEE or KULCHA BIRINJI
Ground rice biscuits   makes about 12

These biscuits are often called *Kulcha Naurozee* because they are specially made for the New Year celebrations, but they are also sometimes made for other festive occasions.

8 oz (225 g) icing sugar
8 oz (225 g) margarine or
  vegetable oil
1 white of an egg
8 oz (225 g) ground rice

1 lb (450 g) plain white flour
1 tsp baking powder or
  bicarbonate of soda
¼ oz (5 g) ground pistachio

If using margarine, melt over a low heat and allow to cool.

Mix the sugar, melted margarine or oil and the white of egg. Sift together the ground rice, plain flour and baking powder, and gradually add to the sugar and margarine mixture, stirring well all the time. Then gently knead until the mixture forms a stiff, smooth dough.

Take a piece of non-stick parchment paper about 6″ by 6″ (15 by 15 cm) and gently roll out on it a piece of dough the size of an egg into the shape of a saucer. Score the biscuit with a fork, forming parallel lines down the biscuit.

Repeat until all the dough has been used up.

Place the biscuits on the parchment papers on baking trays and bake in a preheated oven at 150°C (300°F, mark 2) for 45 minutes. The biscuits should not brown. About 10 minutes before the end of baking time, sprinkle the biscuits lightly with ground pistachio.

When the biscuits are removed they will be crisp. When cool, store in a tin. They will then become softer. Serve the biscuits on the parchment paper.

An Afghan tea-vendor with his samovar

Beverages

TEA

No Afghan cookery book would be complete without mentioning tea, *chai*, which is an important feature of the way of life. It is consumed in great quantities and I must say both the green and black tea are excellent. Afghan tea is particularly refreshing on the hot, dry summer days.

Tea is seldom drunk with milk but is often flavoured with cardamom. On formal occasions, such as weddings and engagements, a special green tea called *qymaq chai* is prepared and drunk. *Qymaq*, which is like clotted cream, is added to the top of the tea. The technique for making *qymaq chai* is elaborate and it has a strong, rich taste; I have given the recipe for it on page 152. Another special tea is *sheer chai*, prepared in the same way but without the *qymaq*. Salt is sometimes added, and it is served with various biscuits or bread such as *roht* or *nan-e-roghani*.

The hospitality of the people can be almost overwhelming at times. A good example of this is the honour attributed to a guest being measured by the amount of sugar he is given with his tea —the more sugar, the more honour. Another Afghan custom is to have a first cup of tea with sugar, *chai shireen*, followed by another cup without sugar. This second cup is called *chai talkh*. Many people soak sugar cubes called *qand* in their tea which they then hold in their mouths as they drink.

Tea is often served with sweets, called *shirnee*, or the Afghan equivalent of sugared almonds, *noql-e-badomi*. *Noql* is also made with roasted chickpeas (*noql-e-nakhodi*) or apricot or peach kernels (sometimes called *noql-e-khastahi*). *Ghur*, a kind of lump sugar made from sugar cane, is also taken with tea, especially in the winter. Another custom often observed is the turning over of your cup when you do not want any more tea. If you fail to do this, the host or hostess will continue to refill your cup with fresh, hot tea.

Because tea plays such an important role there are many *chaikhana*, tea houses, in Afghanistan. Apart from serving tea from a constantly boiling *samovar* they also provide other basic food and requirements for the traveller, for instance a simple and basic soup called *sherwa-e-chainaki*. This soup is actually made in a teapot, hence the name, teapot soup. The tea served in a *chaikhana* can be either black or green and is sometimes served in glass tumblers, but more often in handle-less porcelain bowls, similar to the Chinese tea bowl. Each customer has his own small teapot plus a small bowl for the dregs. When the tea is served, the customer rinses out his glass or bowl with the hot tea and pours this into his dregs bowl. Then he puts sugar, usually quite a lot, into his glass and adds fresh, hot tea. There are no chairs in a *chaikhana* so people sit around, cross-legged, on rugs and carpets on a specially constructed, raised, platform. The walls are also covered with carpets and pictures and there is usually popular Afghan or Indian music playing in the background which can be quite loud.

MILK

Milk is scarce in the cities, and expensive; powdered milk is a common substitute. In the countryside most families maintain at least one goat for producing milk, but without refrigeration this is difficult to keep; so milk products such as yoghurt, *quroot* (p 38), butter and cheese are made. *Qymaq* is a luxury milk product akin to clotted cream (see p 38). A white, uncured round cheese called *kishmish panair* is made in the villages at springtime and brought into the cities for sale; *kishmish* are red raisins, with which this cheese is eaten. (In Baghlan, north of the Hindu Kush, there was a cheese factory which produced some European type cheeses, modelled on Emmenthal, Gouda and Edam.)

A refreshing and popular drink in the summer is *dogh*, a combination of yoghurt, mint, cucumber and salt, for which I give the recipe.

OTHER BEVERAGES

Fruit juices in the summer are made from fresh fruits such as cherries and pomegranates. In winter, lemon and *norinj* (sour orange) are used. The juice of lemon and especially *norinj* are often sprinkled on *chalau* and *pilau* and on salads, for added flavour. In the grape producing areas, for instance north of Kabul, the juice from grapes left over at the end of the season is extracted and kept in a cool place ready for drinking.

Afghanistan is a Muslim country and therefore alcoholic beverages, including wine, are not consumed. However, due to the rich variety and quality of the grapes, a wine factory was set up in the Puli Charkhi area of Kabul in the early 1970s and, with Italian assistance, wines for export were produced.

Beverages

QYMAQ CHAI
Tea with clotted cream   for 4 cups

This is a rich tea, only made for special occasions. It is similar
to Tibetan tea and probably originated there. The Kashmiris
also make a similar tea. However, in Tibet and Kashmir, salt is
added instead of sugar.

Qymaq is the luxury milk product which I have already
described (p 38). Commercial clotted cream can be used as a
substitute although the taste and texture are not quite the
same. Also *qymaq* will float on top of the tea whereas clotted
cream quickly dissolves. Alternatively a combination of a little
qymaq and clotted cream works very well.

24 fl oz (680 ml) water	1-2 tsp ground green or white
6 tsp green tea	cardamom seeds
8 fl oz (225 ml) milk	8 tsp *qymaq* or clotted cream
4-8 tsp sugar	

Put the water in a pan and bring to the boil. Add the green tea
and continue boiling for 5 minutes until the colour of the water
becomes a dark yellow-green. Remove the pan from the heat and
allow the tea leaves to settle. Then strain off the tea into another
pan, removing and discarding the tea leaves. Pour the tea from
one pan to another from a good height—one or two feet!—so
that the tea becomes aerated. Repeat until the colour of the tea
becomes dark red. This may need to be done 20 to 25 times.

Put the pan back on the heat and bring to simmering point.
At the same time bring the milk to simmering point in another
pan. Combine the two. The colour of the tea should then be a
light purple-pink. (In Afghanistan, the best *qymaq chai* was
considered to be the tea which became the colour of the flowers
of the Judas tree in spring. These are purple, like the mountains
which appear deep purply-pink in a certain light and whose
snowy caps are represented by the *qymaq* floating on top of the
tea.) Stir in the sugar and cardamom. Then pour the tea into
individual cups and add two teaspoons of *qymaq* or clotted
cream on top.

This tea is served with *nan-e-roghani* or *kulcha birinji* or just
plain cake or biscuits.

QYMAQ CHAI

Teapot soup

DOGH
Yoghurt and mint drink   serves 6-8

This is an extremely refreshing and relaxing drink on hot, summer days.

1 pint (570 ml) yoghurt
2 pints (1.1 litre) water
5" (13 cm) cucumber, peeled
   and grated (or finely
   chopped)

2 tbs fresh mint, finely
   chopped
1 tsp salt

Add the water to the yoghurt in a large jug. Add the cucumber, fresh mint and salt. Stir well. Keep in the refrigerator until ready to serve.

DOGH

Index

This index gives recipe titles in Dari and English, and also provides references to certain subjects dealt with in the introductory matter.

Index

Index

Measures: Tables of Equivalence

OVEN TEMPERATURES

Fahrenheit	Centigrade	General term and gas-regulo setting	
240	115	very slow	($\frac{1}{4}$)
290	145	slow	(1)
355	180	moderate	(4)
400	205	moderately hot	(6)
430	220	hot	(7)
470	245	very hot	(9)

WEIGHTS

metric	British/U.S.	metric	British/U.S.
10 g	0.36 oz	500 g ($\frac{1}{2}$ kg)	1 lb 1.18 oz
14 g	0.5 oz	567 g	1$\frac{1}{4}$ lb
28 g	1.0 oz	600 g	1 lb 5.4 oz
42 g	1.5 oz	675 g	1$\frac{1}{2}$ lb
50 g	1.8 oz	731 g	1 lb 10.0 oz
56 g	2.0 oz	750 g ($\frac{3}{4}$ kg)	1 lb 10.7 oz
70 g	2.5 oz	785 g	1$\frac{3}{4}$ lb
90 g	3.2 oz	908 g	2 lb
100 g	3.6 oz	1 kg	2 lb 3.7 oz
113 g	4.0 oz ($\frac{1}{4}$ lb)	1 kg 137 g	2$\frac{1}{2}$ lb
126 g	4.5 oz	1$\frac{1}{2}$ kg	3 lb 5.4 oz
150 g	5.3 oz	2 kg	4 lb 7.2 oz
169 g	6.0 oz	2 kg 270 g	5 lb
200 g	7.1 oz	3 kg	6 lb 10.8 oz
227 g	8.0 oz ($\frac{1}{2}$ lb)	3 kg 632 g	8 lb
250 g ($\frac{1}{4}$ kg)	8.9 oz	5 kg	11 lb 2 oz
300 g	10.7 oz		
340 g	12.0 oz ($\frac{3}{4}$ lb)		
397 g	14.0 oz		
454 g	16.0 oz (1 lb)		

MEASURES OF CAPACITY (equivalences between fluid ounces* and millilitres, more exact than those used in the recipes)

metric (ml)	British fl oz*	metric (ml)	British fl oz*
5 (1 tsp)	0.18	196	7
15 (1 tbs)	0.5	227	8
22.5	0.8	250 (¼ litre)	8.9
28	1	280	10
30 (2 tbs)	1.1	336	12
42	1.5	392	14
45 (3 tbs)	1.6	454	16
56	2	500 (½ litre)	17.9
60 (4 tbs)	2.1	560	20
70	2.5	600	21.4
75	2.7	672	24
84	3	750 (¾ litre)	26.8
98	3.5	896	32
112	4	1 litre	35.7
125	4.5	1½ litres	53.6
140	5	2 litres	71.4
150	5.4	2½ litres	89.3
168	6	3 litres	107.1

* The British fluid ounce is fractionally smaller than the U.S. one. This difference, which is of the order of 4%, may be disregarded unless you are dealing with very large quantities.

MEASURES OF CAPACITY (for those still wedded to pints and cups)

British	American	fl oz	metric (ml)
	¼ cup	2	57
¼ cup		2.5	71
	⅓ cup	2.7	76
⅓ cup		3.3	95
	½ cup (¼ pint)	4	113
½ cup (¼ pint)		5	142
	¾ cup	6	170
¾ cup		7.5	198
	1 cup (½ pint)	8	227
1 cup (½ pint)		10	284
	2 cups (1 pint)	16	454
2 cups (1 pint)		20	567
	3 cups	24	680
3 cups		30	850
	4 cups (2 pints)	32	907
4 cups (2 pints)		40	1134